MW00897019

THE
BALANCED MANAGER

BRINGING BOTH EFFICIENCY AND JOY TO THE WORKPLACE

SASS SOMEKH AND ADDI SOMEKH

Copyright © 2009 Sass Somekh and Addi Somekh
All rights reserved.

ISBN: 1-4392-5797-3
ISBN-13: 9781439257975

Visit www.booksurge.com to order additional copies.

Contents

Introduction

The goal of this book is to guide the reader toward becoming a balanced manager - that is, an individual capable of achieving both efficiency and job satisfaction in the workplace.

Fundamental to our approach is the Single-Page concept, which utilizes single pages to understand and constructively analyze key management challenges. The technique enhances the manager's ability to articulate the essence of a problem and prioritize possible solutions. The first nine chapters offer a set of techniques which are all rooted in the Single-Page concept. The last chapter is devoted to practical relationship-skills, as we believe that job satisfaction is greatly enhanced, for both manager and employee, when the manager possesses good interpersonal and relationship building skills.

We present our ideas in the form of a narrative that takes place in the late 1990s, when Sass Somekh was an executive vice president of a multibillion-dollar electronics firm and Addi Somekh had just earned a master's degree in human resource management. Addi's first venture, an ambitious global art project, culminated in the publication of his first book, The Inflatable Crown; his experiences in that process graphically demonstrate the effectiveness of the techniques we describe in the following step-by-step account - in which we alternate as chapter narrators.

Today, Addi is a pioneer in using art as a team-building tool and runs Team Building Arts, a consulting firm with such notable clients as Oprah and Wired magazines, the Disney ABC Network Group, and the Skirball Cultural Center in Los Angeles. Sass Somekh has since been inducted into the Silicon Valley Engineering Hall of Fame for leading the development and business growth of several key products in the semiconductor-equipment industry. Currently he is a co-founder of Musea Ventures, a venture capital firm dedicated to starting and investing in companies in the areas of alternative energy and synthetic biology.

Acknowledgments

We thank Eta and Talli Somekh for their encouragement and support, Rick Hill for suggesting the balanced manager concept, and Mark Graham, whose help in writing the book was invaluable. The comments and suggestions of Riva Brandman, Mendy Erad, Conor Madigan, Pearl O'Brien, Susan Overstreet, Yossi Perl, David Perry, Steve Schwartz and Paula Weigel were extremely helpful in determining the structure and style of this book.

Sass Somekh
Addi Somekh

✧ ✧ ✧

Note: Except for the members of the Somekh family, Charlie Eckert, and Andy Vermouth, all names of individuals and organizations in this book are fictitious.

Chapter 1

Single-Page Personal Plan
Define your ideal jobs and formulate a plan to attain them

"Done!" The sound of my hand pounding the table echoed in the room as I smiled broadly at Mark, head of our mergers and acquisitions group. His team had just completed the strategic acquisition of a software company that I believed would greatly enhance our market position as a leading supplier in the semiconductor industry. As both an executive and his mentor, I had worked closely with Mark as he dealt with the complexities of this challenging negotiation.

Watching this young manager, I reflected upon my own career growth over the past few decades, beginning with my departure from Caltech armed with a Ph.D. in electrical engineering and a burning ambition to succeed. I stood in the conference room as the executive vice president of a multibillion-dollar corporation, responsible for the fortunes of thousands of employees and, more importantly, responsible for the pride, commitment, and passion they brought to their work. I had reached this position through my technical capabilities and an innate ability to organize and lead projects and businesses in the semiconductor industry. An engineer by training, I had developed a reputation as an energetic executive who drives his organization to efficiency and speed - a person who is analytical and direct but not one given to showing much emotion.

Today, however, was different. It was a good day to be a businessman, but it was an even better one to be a father. As I rushed home, I was feeling particularly exhilarated. My high spirits weren't because of the acquisition. I was in an upbeat mood because my son, Addi, had just completed a Master of Arts degree in Human Resource Management, and my wife and I couldn't have been prouder. That was an accomplishment worth celebrating, which was exactly what we were going to do that night.

When I arrived home, I dropped my briefcase in the study and followed the aroma of home cooking toward the kitchen.

"Sass!" Eta stood at the counter putting the finishing touches on Addi's favorite meal. She turned and smiled. "You're home early! How was your day?"

I gave her two thumbs up and said, "We did it. They accepted our price, and we signed the deal an hour ago."

"Congratulations!" Eta wrapped her arms around my neck and gave me a warm hug. She is the glue that holds our family together. Eta is everything I am not - beautiful, funny, and warm - living proof of the old cliché that opposites attract. When I call her Wonder Wife and Super Mom, I really mean it.

"So where's our graduate?" I asked.

"In the Jacuzzi," she answered. "Why don't you join him? I'll bring out a couple of cold beers."

"Sounds great!" And it did. Unwinding in the therapeutic waters of the spa in the company of my older son? Talk about a capital idea.

Addi was floating on his back with his eyes closed as I approached the Jacuzzi, a sight that reminded me of the skinny, black-haired kid who used to beg to stay in the pool "just one more minute," a minute that inevitably turned into thirty. How many times back then had some more experienced mom or dad said to me, "Enjoy these kids, Sass. Time will pass quicker than you think!" And they were right. Now our family spa was not only a place to relax but also a place to connect.

Creative and intuitive, Addi took after his mom. He was an exceptional conversationalist who knew exactly the right question to ask to get people talking, and had the ability to contribute his own insights and observations at the right moment. I always admired the way he could turn a mundane conversation into something special.

I was an engineer. "People skills" did not come easily to me. But when I moved into management, I was forced to learn what my son and wife already knew intuitively.

During his college years, Addi had earned extra spending money working as a balloon artist. He performed at parties and events all over town and now was considered one of the best in the business. It was fascinating to watch him create a hat or a musical instrument from simple pieces of colored latex (think blown-glass art). And it was amazing to see how quickly Addi and his designs could bring a smile to the face of even the most jaded executive.

"Mind if I join you?" I asked, slipping into the Jacuzzi.

Addi opened his eyes and smiled. "Dad! Hey, what's new?"

"Well, we bought that software company I told you about," I said.

"Congrats," he said. "How do you feel about it?"

"Well, it'll be good for both companies when all is said and done," I told him. "But that's not what tonight's about. Tonight, we're celebrating something that's quite a bit more important than a business deal. After all, a master's degree doesn't come along every day!" Then I finished the thought with the kind of zinger that has been putting fear into the hearts of graduates for generations. "So, what are you planning to do with your life, son?"

"Oh, come on!" Addi winced as if good old dad had just opened the Pandora's box of father-son conversations. "The ink has barely dried on my diploma. Are you sure you want to dive into this tonight?"

"There's no time like the present," I answered, with my trademark directness.

It was probably fortunate that Eta walked out with two beers right then, because the last thing I wanted to do was put a damper on our celebration. After she returned to the house, I did a quick about-face and said, "Hey, listen. If you aren't in the mood, we can brainstorm later."

"No. I actually think you're right to say there's no time like the present, because I have something I'd like to discuss with you."

He looked me straight in the eye, and I knew he was serious.

"Okay. I know this is gonna sound a little crazy, but I've been thinking a lot about how successful I've been with my balloon art, and I'd like to take it to another level."

This, I had to admit, was the last thing I expected to hear. I had to force myself not to blurt out, "Is this really the kid I'm hoping to leave a lasting, positive mark on the world?"

Instead, I said, "Okay...Tell me more."

"First of all, I know it's important to think about what my future holds in the long run. But I also think it's just as important to make the most of today. I've always admired how you've built the foundation of a secure life, Dad, and that's a goal we share. Getting a job, starting a career, and all that. And that's where my master's will come in. But as Grandmother Rachel once told me, 'What feeds your heart doesn't necessarily feed your stomach.' And that's what I'm getting at. This will probably be the only time in my life when I'm truly free to take a risk and really test myself. I'm not married. I don't have kids. I'm healthy."

I braced myself, knowing the conversation was veering from the path where I'd hoped it would go but also appreciating what Addi wanted.

"So here's what I'm thinking, Dad," he continued. "I met a photographer in New York recently named Charlie Eckert. He saw my balloon hats and I saw his photography, and we really liked each other's work. One day, we were talking about how bad news always travels faster than good news and how every time we turn on the TV, we're bombarded with the bad news. So we asked ourselves if there might be a way to show that for the most part, people do really get along well."

Addi took a moment to let his words sink in. I had to admit he had my attention. "Okay, and...?"

"And we have this idea of traveling around the world making balloon hats for people and taking photos to see how they react. Because the balloons are nonverbal communicators, like music, they transcend the language barrier. We want to show that all people everywhere are born knowing how to laugh, and we hope to document this point by making a book of photographs of people wearing my hats."

This was not the kind of news a father wants to hear after investing five years worth of pricey tuition in his son's higher education. I could already see Eta in tears and hear her lament: "My son is going to join the circus."

"Maybe the notion of a long-term social experiment involving balloon hats and the effect they can have on different cultures sounds crazy, but I'm serious about this, Dad."

"Yes, I can see that, Addi," I said, warning myself to tread lightly. "And you know I've always encouraged you to do something you love and do it to the best of your ability."

"And I've always appreciated the encouragement."

"So my question is: Are you willing to put this idea into a business model? Something a businessman like myself can look at and evaluate, and something that will force you to take a realistic look at your idea?"

"Well, seeing as how you didn't faint or cut me off, I guess I can hear you out," Addi said with some relief. "What do you have in mind?"

"It's a technique I've developed over the years called the Single-Page Personal Plan, or SP3. The idea is to help you define - on a simple piece of paper - your ideal jobs and to formulate a plan to attain them. Here's how it works. I sat up and said, "Imagine three slightly overlapping circles. Circle one represents your strengths. Circle two, the things you enjoy doing. And circle three, your long-term goals. The best, most ideal jobs are the ones we find where these three circles - our strengths, passions, and long-term goals - intersect. I call it the 'Personal Fulfillment Triangle.' Finding your triangle will help you evaluate whether or not to pursue this project you have in mind."

"I'll give it a try," said Addi.

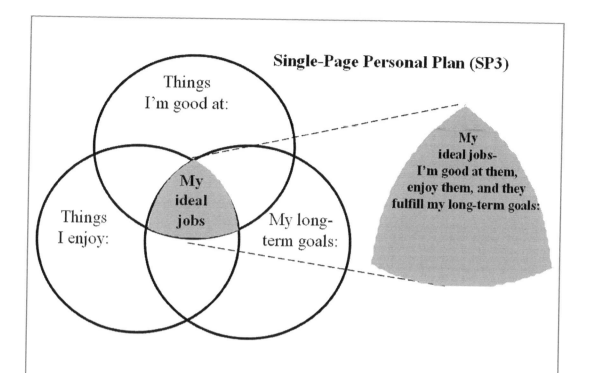

1. SUCCESS CRITERIA (measurable and scheduled accomplishments over the next 5 years aimed at attaining an ideal job)

2. PROBLEM STATEMENT (obstacles to success)

3. STRATEGIES (plans to overcome the obstacles)

4. DELIVERABLES OVER THE NEXT 12 MONTHS (specific items, dates)

Download at www.TheBalancedManager.com

Addi looked at the form and smiled politely. My son was not the kind to enjoy figuring out crossword puzzles, much less completing questionnaires or surveys. In college, he even stressed out about something as routine as an application form.

After we talked about it for a few minutes I said: "You know as well as I do that taking a job that you know you'd be good at but wouldn't enjoy doesn't make sense, right? And it also doesn't make much sense to consider a job you might enjoy but don't have the skills for."

"Not to mention trying to achieve my long-term goals at this stage of life," he said. "So what about jobs that don't fall within the intersection of the three circles? Like jobs that only overlap at two circles?"

"Well, doing a job you're good at and one that supports your goals is a good way to start. But you have to ask yourself how long you'd last if you didn't enjoy it."

"Right. And taking a job I enjoy and that supports my long-term goals but that I am not good at would be frustrating," Addi said.

"Exactly," I replied. "And while finding something you're good at and enjoy might sound like fun, you have to ask yourself how long the fun would last if you aren't meeting your long-term goals."

"Yeah, kind of an extended childhood." Addi grinned.

"Look, I know what you're thinking: My dad wants me to fill out a form that's supposed to help me plan out the rest of my life. He must be kidding!"

As I headed out the door for my regular Saturday morning hike, I called over my shoulder one last bit of advice. "Don't over-think it."

"Who, me? Over-think something?" Addi laughed.

The Single-Page Personal-Plan (SP3) was simple and straightforward, but he still tried to find a flaw in it that would allow him to take a pass. Admittedly, however, there was something appealing about the prospect of combining what he was good at with what he enjoyed and then overlapping these with his long-term goals.

Then, with a pencil in hand and my advice about not over-thinking in mind, Addi started jotting notes, which he then copied onto the SP3 form. He filled in the three circles labeled: Things I'm good at, Things I enjoy, and My long-term goals. Then he focused on his success criteria, problem statement, and deliverables over a twelve-month period.

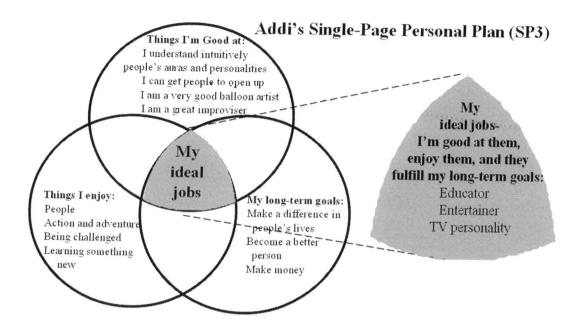

Addi's Single-Page Personal Plan (SP3)

Things I'm Good at:
I understand intuitively
people's auras and personalities
I can get people to open up
I am a very good balloon artist
I am a great improviser

My ideal jobs

Things I enjoy:
People
Action and adventure
Being challenged
Learning something
new

My long-term goals:
Make a difference in
people's lives
Become a better
person
Make money

My
ideal jobs—
I'm good at them,
enjoy them, and they
fulfill my long-term goals:
Educator
Entertainer
TV personality

1. **SUCCESS CRITERIA** (measurable and scheduled accomplishments over the next 5 years aimed at attaining an ideal job)

- Travel to various locations worldwide, making balloon hats for people and documenting the results with professional-quality photos.
- Publish a book of these photos that:
    - Will demonstrate that all human beings are born knowing how to laugh and experience joy
    - Will enable Charlie and me to leverage the project to secure one of our "ideal jobs"

2. **PROBLEM STATEMENT** (obstacles to success)

- Uncharted territory: Because this sort of project has not been done before, there's no one to provide advice.
- Not entirely sure that Charlie and I will get along as well as I anticipate.
- No money to fund the various aspects of the project, including travel.
- No contacts in the publishing or entertainment worlds.

3. **STRATEGIES** (plans to overcome the obstacles)

- Make a trial run aimed at finding out:
    - If the material is suitable for a book by contacting several qualified publishers
    - If Charlie and I can cooperate well enough to create a great product;
- Look for foundations that support the arts and see if any might be willing to sponsor such a project.
- Use research and family connections to identify contacts in publishing and entertainment.

4. **DELIVERABLES OVER THE NEXT TWELVE MONTHS** (specific items, dates)

- Plan and execute a short trip to Central America within three months.
- Identify a suitable foundation and secure commitment for funding within six months.
- Identify at least one publisher with an interest in a book, ideally within the next twelve months.
- Embark on one major trip within nine months.
- Complete the first major trip within twelve months.

When I returned from my hike, Addi was waiting in my study.

"So how did it go?" I asked.

"I have to admit the Single-Page Personal Plan is an effective tool," he replied.

I read his completed SP3 and smiled at the results.

"Well?" Addi asked.

"The good news is it looks great."

"And the bad news?"

"Now I have to break it to mom that you might be embarking on a global balloon-twisting journey."

Chapter 2

Single-Page Positioning Method
Articulate the essence of any subject

Dad was right. Filling out his Single-Page Personal Plan wasn't so bad. In fact, I actually enjoyed it. The process forced me to think, plan, and prioritize, and I found I was pretty good at all three once I got going. On a single page, I could bring focus to my aspirations in a way I hadn't considered before.

But now that I'd completed the SP3, the hard part began. It was easy to dream yet it would be hard to turn those dreams into something real.

And reality, not surprisingly, began with money.

I spent the next few days in the library and online. I listed everything Charlie and I would need for our project - from balloons and plane tickets to camera equipment and a new computer - and estimated how much all of it would likely cost. I tried to be as realistic as possible and finally determined that food, ground transportation, travel documents, and inoculations would bring the total to about $100,000.

Then I searched the Internet for potential foundation sponsorship, and narrowed the list to three: the Orange County Foundation of the Arts, Mission World, and the Jerry James Foundation, a nonprofit dedicated to sponsoring artists and arts organizations. I put the latter foundation at the top of my list and read everything I could about it, learning who its founders were, what its mission statement espoused, whom it had sponsored in the past and was currently sponsoring and, finally, what sums it had granted to date.

The nagging question in my mind was how a balloon artist would ever be able to convince a well-established nonprofit such as the Jerry James Foundation to put up such a large sum of money to support the unconventional project Charlie and I were proposing.

On the following Saturday, Dad's hiking day, I decided to join him and use our time together to pick his brain.

We set out from the house far earlier than any self-respecting night owl - namely, me - would under normal circumstances. But these circumstances weren't normal. I had taken the first step in pursuit of an important personal goal, and I was eager to see where it might lead.

We hit the trail at a brisk pace. For the first fifteen minutes or so, there wasn't much talk; Dad focused on his breathing, and I focused on keeping up. By the time we were both huffing and puffing, I suggested, "Why don't we take five and enjoy the view?"

We got out our water bottles and caught our breath. I decided this was as good a time as any to broach the subject of my project. "By the way," I began, "I've been researching a foundation I think might be right for funding our trip, and I'm trying to figure out the best way to approach the powers-that-be and convince them to support us. I thought you might have some ideas."

"Absolutely." Dad nodded up the trail, and we started walking again, though at a more leisurely pace. I knew he was organizing his thoughts. He was as analytical and organized as I was spontaneous and creative, which was one reason I respected his point of view as much as I did. Eventually, he said, "Think about your daily experiences and the situations in which other people are trying to convince *you* to do things."

I thought for a minute, and smiled. "You mean like TV commercials - the art of convincing us to buy things we might not buy otherwise?"

"Exactly," Dad said. "So let's take car commercials. Think about how they affect us and influence us. For me, the most effective ads are the ones that focus on a particular feature I happen to be interested in. But the commercial doesn't just brag about this feature; it actually *proves* it."

"Remember that commercial for the Lexus 400, the one with the wine glasses all stacked up on the hood? They were demonstrating how quiet and vibration-free the car was, and that's what hooked me. I went right out and test drove the 400."

I had to smile. "Okay, so here's a guy who's been driving an MGB convertible for years, and all of a sudden you're hooked on quiet and vibration-free driving?"

"Yeah, can you believe it? But that was also about the time fairly decent car phones were becoming available. I used to call our office in Europe on the way to work and our office in Japan on the road back home. So a quiet environment was important to me."

He shrugged and added, "But you're right. Did I really need it so quiet and vibration-free that you could stack wine glasses on the hood without breaking them? Not likely. But one of the key aspects of the art of advertising is taking the positive attributes of your product and promoting them as if they were the most important things of all. So tell me, what's your favorite car commercial?"

"Well, I really don't care much about car commercials," I said, "but I can see how that BMW ad, the one that combined the 'ultimate driving machine' slogan with the guy blasting along a winding mountain road, would be effective. On the other hand, it's just a catchy phrase and some great action footage."

"The result," Dad explained, "is called 'positioning.' BMW - 'The ultimate driving machine' - and Lexus - 'The pursuit of perfection.' Lexus makes its point by using wine glasses to prove its claim, while BMW achieves a similar effect but with exhilarating driving footage."

"So what you're saying is that I'll need to provide any potential sponsor with plenty of 'proof' to support our unconventional project. Like a portfolio of fascinating pictures of my balloons in action and maybe some really good stories to verify the claim. Right?"

"Exactly."

"I realize now it would also be a good idea to come up with a catchy phrase to 'position' the project."

"Something that will capture the imagination of the foundation people." Dad said "Something that will occur to them every time they think of your project. So are you ready to tackle your next single page?"

"If it works as well as the SP3, definitely," I said, scarcely able to believe my enthusiasm and curiosity. "What's this one about?"

"I call it the SPPM, for Single-Page Positioning Method."

After our hike, Dad gave me the form, and I began crafting my responses according to the specifics of Charlie's and my project. I was fast becoming a fan of the Single-Page concept, which was simple, concise, and direct. As I filled in the SPPM's five sections, I didn't over think the process. Instead, I wrote down, as quickly as possible, one-word descriptors of the project Charlie and I were developing.

Then I slowed down, as I began prioritizing those attributes - first, as they would influence our "customers" first, and then how they would distinguish us from our "competition." This was a valuable exercise, because it made me focus on my intended audience, which eventually inspired me to create a catchy tag line.

Single-Page Positioning Method (SPPM)

1. LIST THE ATTRIBUTES OF WHAT YOU WANT TO POSITION (your product, your company, yourself, etc.)

2. PRIORITIZE THE LIST (according to the impact on the people you wish to influence or your "customers")

3. REPRIORITIZE TO DIFFERENTIATE YOURSELF FROM YOUR "COMPETI-TORS" (those who vie for the same influence on your "customers")

4. CAPTURE THE ESSENCE OF THE TOP ATTRIBUTES IN A SINGLE SENTENCE

5. SIMPLIFY YOUR MESSAGE (reduce the number of words while keeping it catchy and memorable)

Download at www.TheBalancedManager.com

Single-Page Positioning Method (SPPM)
The Balloon Hat Project

1. **LIST THE ATTRIBUTES OF WHAT YOU WANT TO POSITION** (your product, your company, yourself, etc.)

Unique	Funny
Feel Good	Beautiful
Universal	Wearable Art
Happiness	Inflatable
Good News	Ground Breaking
Crown	Soon-to-be-Classic
Global	Balloon Twister
Laughing	Collaboration
All Ages	Antidote to Bad News
Cross Boundaries	Smiling

2. **PRIORITIZE THE LIST** (according to the impact on the people you wish to influence or your "customers")

Unique	Happiness
Beautiful	Good News
Crown	Smiling
Wearable Art	Cross Boundaries
Laughing	Inflatable
Global	Ground Breaking
All Ages	Soon-to-be-Classic
Feel Good	Balloon Twister
Funny	Collaboration
Universal	Antidote to Bad News

3. **REPRIORITIZE TO DIFFERENTIATE YOURSELF FROM YOUR "COMPETITORS"** (those who vie for the same influence on your "customers")

Other people applying for the same grant will surely have similar themes, so I realized I should stress aspects of the project that will distinguish our proposal from everyone else's. I reviewed the list and narrowed it down:

Inflatable	Happiness
Balloon	Laughing
Wearable Art	All Ages

4. **CAPTURE THE ESSENCE OF THE TOP ATTRIBUTES IN A SINGLE SENTENCE**

With this newly prioritized list, I tried to come up with my own tagline or slogan. I thought of a few classic ad slogans that were etched in my mind: "7 Up, the Uncola," or "Don't squeeze the Charmin," or "You're in good hands with Allstate."

First try: "Twist and Shout - Pumping up Smiles around the World"

Second try: "The Balloon Twister's Guide to Universal Happiness"

Third try: "The Inflatable Crown - Offering Proof That Laughter Sounds the Same in Every Language"

5. **SIMPLIFY YOUR MESSAGE** (reduce the number of words while keeping it catchy and memorable)

"The Inflatable Crown - Laughter Sounds the Same in Every Language"

I felt good about distilling the essence of the idea into a catchy phrase that would be easy to explain. I especially liked the concept of an "inflatable crown." Throughout the ages and in almost all cultures, headdresses have identified the unique qualities of a people and signified their distinguishing ethnic characteristics. Crowns have always been the quintessential manifestation of this universal form of expression. The term *inflatable* added a note of modernity to the subject, made the crown "larger than life" in new ways, and infused the idea with a sense of fun and buoyancy.

I studied my Single-Page Personal Plan alongside my newly filled-out Single-Page Positioning Method. Then I took both pages to my desk and looked at them in conjunction with the research notes I had made for our project. I added my budget to the mix and was surprised at how far I had come. I was feeling more confident about the project because I had thought out and written down a personal plan and I had defined how I intended to proceed. But there were still several big questions - sketched out on the SP3 - that I needed to answer before I could begin to seek funding in earnest:

1. Would Charlie and I get along well enough to create a powerful partnership, one that would enhance our goals rather than stifle them? I felt confident we would, but it was essential to test that hunch before we set out on a long trip that was bound to be stressful, no matter what.

2. Would people in various cultures really like my balloon art? Would it capture their imaginations and elicit the kind of joyful response I most often saw when entertaining people here in the States?

3. Would the response to our photos of audiences in the States be sufficient to entice potential publishers to acquire our book?

Charlie and I met in a coffee shop the next day. We discussed the results of my efforts to date and thrashed out answers to the three questions that I felt needed to be resolved.

"We need to make a test run," Charlie said, as if nothing could be more obvious. "Let's head down to Central America for four or five weeks to see how things go. We'll plan it out just like we would the longer venture. My mom's a flight attendant, so we can get tickets nearly for free. We'll visit a dozen or so places. You'll make your balloon hats, and I'll snap pictures until my fingers fall off."

"And we come home with the 'proof' we need for our grant," I added.

"Exactly."

It wasn't as simple as that, of course, but we organized the trip in less than a month, laying out a five-week itinerary that included travel in Guatemala, Honduras, and Nicaragua. Charlie's mom came through on the plane tickets, and we set out with the gear we required, including a backpack filled with balloons.

Here's a summary of the trip, extracted from my journal:

We decided on Central America for a couple of reasons. For one, we both spoke enough Spanish to get around and not get lost at the bus station. For another, Charlie had traveled there once before.

We decided to fly into Guatemala and then travel through Honduras into Nicaragua. Almost all of Central America had been embroiled in civil wars during the 1980s - the main exception being Costa Rica - and things were just beginning to stabilize in the countries we were visiting. Charlie and I prepared by reading books about the politics that had contributed to the turmoil.

We landed in Guatemala City, with a population of six million, and spent just enough time there to get our bearings - exchange money, study maps, and figure out bus schedules.

A six-hour bus ride took us to an elevation of 8,000 feet and the Mayan village of Todos Santos Cuchumatán, where we spent a week. We each lived with a different family, taking Spanish-language classes during the day. Of course, most of our time was spent walking around and making balloon hats for people and taking photos of them. In fact, our first experiment was so successful that we had to leave because we were too popular. Every day, more and more people sought us out, coming to the homes of the families we were staying with and demanding that I make more balloons art!

Our next stop was the coast of Honduras, where we made balloon hats for Garifuna fisherman and their families. Another huge success.

So far, so good. Charlie and I made a good team, we genuinely got along, and everybody loved the balloons. The most sensitive part of the trip, however, was still to come.

We headed to Nicaragua. The United States was implicated in the chaos that had torn that country apart. That meant we had no idea how people would receive us. As my friend Bill once told me about his military service in Vietnam, "Hope for the best, expect the worst and be ready for both."

We took a bus to the capital, Managua, and hung out there for a couple days, trying to determine the best places to go to make balloon hats by talking with travelers and locals. We visited León, a city where some of the heaviest fighting had occurred; bullet holes pockmarked at least half the buildings there. Thankfully, people greeted us with respect and were happy to have balloon hats made for them.

We next went to Bluefields, a city on Nicaragua's Caribbean coast. A two-night bus ride got us there, and we hired a small motorboat to take us into the jungle, where came upon a remote village of Mosquito Indians. As I began making balloon hats for some of the children, one of the elders came up to Charlie and said: "You don't know how important it is for the children to see these hats and to wear them. These are very similar to the hats our ancestors wore, hats made from the feathers of birds that are no longer here."

Our goal had simply been to make people laugh and be happy. It took us entirely by surprise to see that something as simple and ephemeral as a balloon hat could help a community connect with its own history.

We returned home after five weeks, feeling as though we'd succeeded on at least two counts. For one, Charlie and I were able to work together even better than I had hoped, complementing each other's skills as well as finding a comfortable balance in the way we communicated. For another, everyone we met had been crazy about the balloon hats!

We spent the next week developing Charlie's photos, and the response to them was more gratifying than either of us could have imagined. Even those who were skeptical about our project were fascinated by the images.

Now that we could confidently call our test run an unqualified success, Charlie and I decided to ramp things up for our major around-the-world journey. This decision, as it turned out, prompted me to take the next step in my father's Single-Page approach.

Chapter 3

Quarter-Page Synopsis
Capture reader attention with structure and brevity

The experience gained from our five weeks in Central America and the quality of the photographs we had brought home gave me even more confidence about moving forward with the full project - a worldwide trip that would take us to four continents and thirty-four countries. I also felt it was time to approach the Jerry James Foundation and request the necessary $100,000 grant.

Needless to say, I didn't expect to encounter quite so soon what was sure to be the first of many hurdles in the process. When I called the foundation to explore the best way to submit a grant proposal, the person I reached informed me that the organization didn't review unsolicited applications. No exceptions. This was disappointing news, especially coming on the heels of the great high I had been feeling after the trip. My first thought was to drop the foundation idea and explore other funding options. Instead, I decided to talk it over with Dad and get his take on the situation.

"Where do things stand?" he asked as we chatted in his study.

"I just learned that the Jerry James Foundation won't accept unsolicited applications. So I'm thinking I may have to look elsewhere."

"Listen, Addi, if you're going to travel the world doing something no one has done before, you're going to encounter obstacles more difficult than one person blocking your way," he replied. "Which means you're going to have to learn to be a lot more resourceful and persistent than a single phone call. Have you written an introductory letter to the foundation?"

"Not yet," I admitted.

"Why don't you start there," he said, "and then let me take a look. As you know, I'm always good for an opinion or two."

"Really, Dad? Since when?" I teased.

I spent the next two hours drafting a letter to the foundation. Remember, I had just come from graduate school, where lengthy, even long-winded essays were considered a high form of communication. And that was exactly the way I wrote the first draft of my letter.

I handed the three-page document to Dad the next morning. He shook his head. "Too long. Way too long." He read it anyway.

When finished he said: "You express yourself well. You always have. But in order to have a serious impact in the business world, Addi, you have to be much more concise and direct."

"Yeah, I know. Way too wordy."

"I have an interesting example that will show you what I mean about impact," he said. He handed two pages to me, and I was immediately struck by the historic significance of the document I was holding. It was a letter Albert Einstein wrote to President Franklin D. Roosevelt in August 1939.

Albert Einstein
Old Grove Rd.
Nassau Point
Peconic, Long Island

August 2nd, 1939

F.D. Roosevelt,
President of the United States,
White House
Washington, D.C.

Sir:

Some recent work by E. Fermi and L. Szilard, which has been communicated to me in manuscript, leads me to expect that the element uranium may be turned into a new and important source of energy in the immediate future. Certain aspects of the situation which has arisen seem to call for watchfulness and, if necessary, quick action on the part of the Administration. I believe therefore that it is my duty to bring to your attention the following facts and recommendations:

In the course of the last four months it has been made probable - through the work of Joliot in France as well as Fermi and Szilard in America - that it may become possible to set up a nuclear chain reaction in a large mass of uranium, by which vast amounts of power and large quantities of new radium-like elements would be generated. Now it appears almost certain that this could be achieved in the immediate future.

This new phenomenon would also lead to the construction of bombs, and it is conceivable - though much less certain - that extremely powerful bombs of a new type may thus be constructed. A single bomb of this type, carried by boat and exploded in a port, might very well destroy the whole port together with some of the surrounding territory. However, such bombs might very well prove to be too heavy for transportation by air.

The United States has only very poor ores of uranium in moderate quantities. There is some good ore in Canada and the former Czechoslovakia, while the most important source of uranium is Belgian Congo.

In view of this situation you may think it desirable to have some permanent contact maintained between the Administration and the group of physicists working on chain reactions in America. One possible way of achieving this might be for you to entrust with this task a person who has your confidence and who could perhaps serve in an inofficial capacity. His task might comprise the following:

a) to approach Government Departments, keep them informed of the further development, and put forward recommendations for Government action, giving particular attention to the problem of securing a supply of uranium ore for the United States;

b) to speed up the experimental work,which is at present being carried on within the limits of the budgets of University laboratories, by providing funds, if such funds be required, through his contacts with private persons who are willing to make contributions for this cause, and perhaps also by obtaining the co-operation of industrial laboratories which have the necessary equipment.

I understand that Germany has actually stopped the sale of uranium from the Czechoslovakian mines which she has taken over. That she should have taken such early action might perhaps be understood on the ground that the son of the German Under-Secretary of State, von Weizsäcker, is attached to the Kaiser-Wilhelm-Institut in Berlin where some of the American work on uranium is now being repeated.

Yours very truly,

A. Einstein

(Albert Einstein)

"What do you think?" Dad asked.

"Amazing."

"Now, take a few minutes to analyze the writing - one paragraph at a time."

As I did, I jotted down observations in the margins:

- The first two paragraphs focus on background information on the new phenomenon of nuclear energy. The second paragraph amplifies more recent developments, giving that passage a sense of immediacy.

- The third and last paragraph on the first page describes the awesome opportunity this technology might offer when applied to the manufacture of bombs. Interestingly, Einstein is careful not to over-promise on this opportunity, noting that it is "much less certain" that an extremely powerful bomb can be constructed.

- Most of the second page consists of a detailed proposal for how the U.S. government should address this opportunity. It starts with uranium ore availability, suggests the appointment of a trusted individual to monitor and perhaps expedite for the project, and concludes with the prospect of supporting research in universities.

- The closing paragraph highlights the importance and timeliness of the opportunity by strongly suggesting that the Germans are already acting on it.

I noted, "The last paragraph sort of says, 'Hey, Mr. President, this is for real, and if you don't believe me, just watch what the Germans are doing!'"

"Nothing like a little competitive threat to light a fire under people."

"So what happened? Did President Roosevelt 'get it' instantly and immediately launch the actions requested by Einstein?"

"He got it immediately, all right," Dad answered, handing me a copy of Roosevelt's response. "Take a look."

The letter was brief and to the point, describing the immediate action taken. It was impossible to miss the impact Einstein's letter had had on the thirty-second president of the United States.

THE WHITE HOUSE
WASHINGTON

October 19, 1939

My dear Professor:

I want to thank you for your recent letter and the most interesting and important enclosure.

I found this data of such import that I have convened a Board consisting of the head of the Bureau of Standards and a chosen representative of the Army and Navy to thoroughly investigate the possibilities of your suggestion regarding the element of uranium.

I am glad to say that Dr. Sachs will cooperate and work with this Committee and I feel this is the most practical and effective method of dealing with the subject.

Please accept my sincere thanks.

Very sincerely yours,

Franklin D. Roosevelt

Dr. Albert Einstein,
Old Grove Road,
Nassau Point,
Peconic, Long Island,
New York.

After reading Roosevelt's response, I said: "History aside, that's exactly the kind of positive response I'd like to get from the Jerry James Foundation. I know you're leading up to something, Dad, and I'm hoping it'll work as well as the Single-Page Personal Plan and the Single-Page Positioning Method."

"As a matter of fact, I think it will," he said, handing me another page. "Here you'll find some of the same features you saw in the Einstein letter, with one major exception. In today's business environment, peoples' attention spans are short. We live in a bullet-point world, and it's very likely people will read your letter on their Blackberries and make decisions on the elevator. I call this the QPS, for Quarter-Page Synopsis. It should help you get attention by delivering your message quickly, succinctly, and clearly. See what you think, and let me know when you're done."

Quarter-Page Synopsis (QPS)

1. The purpose of the QPS is to get attention.
2. Keep it short - a quarter page or less.
3. Make it easy to read and understand.
4. Frame it using the Problem/Benefit/Solution/Proof format:
    a. Start by giving a background if required.
    b. Describe the problem/opportunity.
    c. Describe the benefits of solving the problem/pursuing the opportunity.
    d. Describe the proposed solution.
    e. Conclude, if possible, with a proof that the solution indeed works.

Download at www.TheBalancedManager.com

As I read the form, I told myself to keep my "responses" brief - to dedicate no more than two or three sentences to the problem, the benefit, the proposed solution, and the proof. I started writing. Two drafts later, I felt I'd achieved my goal.

The Inflatable Crown - Laughter Sounds the Same in Every Language

Why is it that every time we watch the news, we only seem to hear what is going wrong in the world? Could something as simple as a balloon hat show that the world is not as troubled as we're led to believe?

Two young American artists might have an unexpected and uplifting answer. Addi Somekh is a balloon artist who improvises headdresses to reflect the wearer's personality. Charlie Eckert possesses the skills of a photojournalist and the sensitivity of a portrait photographer.

Together, the two travel the world, surprising people with improvised balloon "crowns" and documenting the reactions elicited by the headdresses. The magic of the balloon hats works as a language without words, transcending boundaries and allowing strangers to become friends quickly. The photos Charlie takes of these encounters are both amusing and uplifting, and they challenge the steady stream of bad news and stereotypes.

I ran this by Dad, and he agreed it fit his criteria for a successful Quarter-Page Synopsis.

The next step was to see if the people at the Jerry James Foundation would react as positively as I hoped. That afternoon, I made a beautiful balloon flower using the same colors featured in the foundation's logo - green, yellow, and white. Then I chose one of my favorite photographs from our trip to Central America: an image of a smiling six-year-old girl from a Honduran village wearing a towering balloon hat that looked like a colorful castle.

I jumped in my car and headed for San Francisco. The foundation's headquarters were just east of Union Square. I parked nearby and walked through the front door with my balloon flower in one hand and a folder containing the photo and my QPS in the other.

"Good afternoon," I said to the receptionist. "I'm Addi Somekh. I'm with the Inflatable Crown project."

"What a beautiful flower," she said, taking in my balloon creation. "Did you make that?"

"Yes, I did." I showed her the photo. "My partner and I have been all over Central America, making inflatable hats for people and collecting photographs for a book we hope to publish."

"Adorable," she said, looking at the little girl's hat and the smile it had produced.

"I wanted to see if I could arrange a short meeting with your executive director. I don't have an appointment, but it would only take a few minutes," I said.

"I'm sorry, but Mr. Page is out. He'll be back in the morning."

"Would you mind if I left these for him?" I asked, holding out the balloon flower, the photograph, and the QPS.

"Not at all," she replied. "I'll put them on his desk right now and make sure he sees them first thing. I'll let you know what he says."

She exchanged the flower and the file for one of Charles Page's business cards.

It hadn't gone exactly as I had hoped, but at least I'd gotten my foot in the door.

Chapter 4

Single-Page Visit
Plan your visits to achieve your goals

I could hear the excitement in Addi's voice when he called me at the office just before lunchtime.

"What's up?" I asked.

"I wanted to let you know I just got a call from the Jerry James Foundation. Charles Page, the executive director got my package, and his secretary called to say he was impressed with the flower I made and the information I shared on the QPS."

"Excellent news," I said. "That's the kind of response we were talking about. So what's next?"

"Even though they don't normally accept unsolicited applications," Addi said, "the executive director is going to make an exception." I could hear a hint of pride in his voice. He had been able to break through what seemed to be a roadblock, and suddenly the prospect of raising the money for his travels looked more realistic. "Mr. Page wants to meet with me the day after tomorrow."

My son was seeing how a well-executed plan can produce desirable results. Now, if he could just keep the momentum going.

We continued our conversation that evening. I began by asking,

"Have you thought about your plan for the meeting?" I didn't want Addi to assume that just because a meeting was scheduled, he didn't have to keep strategizing. This was no time for overconfidence or complacency.

"Do I hear a well-meaning and sage piece of advice headed my way?" he joked. "Go for it, Dad."

"To quote General Dwight D. Eisenhower, 'Plans are nothing; *planning* is everything.'"

"Come on!" Addi laughed. "It's just going to be a meeting, not the invasion of Europe."

"But it'll be an important meeting that could have a major impact on your project, right?" I answered. I didn't want this lesson to fall on deaf ears. Experience told me this could be one of those critical moments in Addi's evolution as a businessman. "A meeting you want to make sure you 'win,' right?"

"Of course, I want to make sure it's a 'win,' Dad," he said. "That's the whole idea. But that's not how I operate. You know as well as I do that I have confidence in my ability to assess situations and improvise accordingly. I have no problem making a judgment about the circumstances and the people involved, and then letting my instincts guide me."

"I'm not arguing against your instincts. Your instincts and your ability to think and act on your feet have always been among your strong suits. I just want you to see how planning can enhance those strengths."

At that moment, Charlie arrived with a camera slung over each shoulder and wearing his usual affable smile. I invited him to join the conversation, telling him we needed a third opinion.

"I know you're a longtime New York Giants fan," I began. Do you know of any football team that has been successful simply by improvising its plays?"

"Not really," he replied. "Improvisation gets you only so far. That's what game planning is all about."

"Which is why coaches spend so much time in the film room and just as much time putting together their game plan, right?"

Addi and I had taken in many San Francisco 49ers games in the team's heyday during the 1980s and early 1990s, and we enjoyed reminiscing about how great they had once been.

"As a matter of fact," said Charlie, "your Niners were known to have their first twenty offensive plays scripted long before kickoff. The coach, Bill Walsh, and his staff would watch film of their upcoming opponent and know exactly what they wanted to do in their first series of drives. With the flawless execution of Joe Montana, the quarterback, it worked very well for them."

"True," Addi said. "But let's not forget their defense. If I recall, they weren't half bad either. And if I also recall, some of those players thrived on improvisation and snap decisions."

"Can't argue with that," said Charlie. "The best teams have both - a great offense *and* a strong defense."

"The same applies to business," I said, using the analogy to segue back to our discussion about planning and preparation. "The strongest leaders are those who are capable of planning well, executing well, and changing and adjusting when the situation requires it. The same goes for companies as a whole. They create a strategy, they figure out the best tactics to execute that strategy, and then they monitor their progress objectively, making judgments and adjustments as necessary."

"In other words," Addi said, "Eisenhower was right: Plans are nothing; *planning* is everything."

Needless to say, I was preparing to give Addi the next of my single pages. When I handed him my Single-Page Visit (SPV) to help him prepare for his meeting at the Jerry James Foundation, I think he was already curious to see it.

"This one will take some thought and research," I told him. "Some of the facts - such as who, what, and where - you already know. But you'll need to gather more background information."

"The fewer surprises, the better," Addi said.

"That's right," I said, and then pointed to number five on the Single-Page Visit form: Success Criteria. "Don't be shy about setting your success criteria, but also be realistic. What do you expect out of the meeting? What would convince you the meeting had been a success?"

Without waiting for an answer, I pointed to number six, the Problem Statement. "You want to go into your meeting knowing there are always problems to overcome in achieving your success criteria. I suggest, then, that you think about what those might be."

Addi nodded and said, "And number seven is about coming up with plans to overcome those possible obstacles."

"Yes. And number eight prompts you to think about some of the actions you might need to take before the meeting. Finally, you'll fill in number nine right after the meeting, as a summary and a reminder of the agreed-upon action items."

"Thanks, Dad. We'll start working on it now."

Charlie gave Addi his input regarding their success criteria and the problems their potential sponsors might have in supporting such an unusual project. Then they brainstormed possible strategies Addi could use during the meeting.

"You're sure you don't want me to attend the meeting with you?" Charlie asked.

"Why don't we start this as a one-on-one meeting," Addi replied. "I'll talk about you and introduce your photographs as part of the pitch. If the meeting gets us a follow up, we'll go in as a team."

Single-Page Visit (SPV)

1. ORGANIZATION, VISIT LOCATION, DATE, TIME

2. BACKGROUND

3. ORGANIZATION'S PARTICIPANTS (their backgrounds, positions, responsibilities and authority to make decision affecting us; interest in the visit and feeling toward us and our competitors; personality type of each - driver or amiable, innovative or analytical)

4. OUR PARTICIPANTS

5. SUCCESS CRITERIA (desired outcome of the visit in terms of achieving measurable results)

6. PROBLEM STATEMENT (possible obstacles to success)

7. STRATEGIES TO BE USED DURING THE VISIT (plans to overcome the possible obstacles)

8. ACTIONS TO COMPLETE BEFORE THE VISIT

9. AFTER THE VISIT: SUMMARY AND ACTION ITEMS (have we met our success criteria?)

Download at www.TheBalancedManager.com

Single-Page Visit (SPV)

1. **ORGANIZATION, VISIT LOCATION, DATE, TIME**
   Jerry James Foundation -
   1870 Jackson Avenue, San Francisco, CA 94109
   February 5, 9 a.m.

2. **BACKGROUND:**
   The Jerry James Foundation is a non-profit dedicated to sponsoring artists and art organizations. We have found out that they do not accept unsolicited applications, but Page Smith has agreed to take the meeting. While they are a reasonably large foundation with a diversified portfolio, we have not been able to find cases in which they have granted $100K.

3. **ORGANIZATION PARTICIPANTS (their backgrounds, positions, responsibilities and authority to make decision affecting us; interest in the visit and feeling toward us and competitors; personality type of each - driver or amiable, innovative or analytical)**
   - Charles Page, Executive Director - according to the official foundation bio, he has a master's degree in nonprofit management. Early in his career, he did a three-year tour of duty with the Peace Corps in Africa; this could bode well for the Inflatable Crown project's travel criteria. Mr. Page is married with two daughters.

4. **OUR PARTICIPANT**
   - Addi Somekh

5. **SUCCESS CRITERIA (desired outcome of the visit in terms of achieving measurable results)**
   - To have Charles Page write a check for $100,000 on the spot, or at least to have the Inflatable Crown project put on track to receive funding.

6. **PROBLEM STATEMENT (possible obstacles to success)**
   - Mr. Page might not consider balloon art worthy of funding.
   - He might consider our project an unproven idea with inherent risks.
   - He might dismiss The Inflatable Crown project as just two guys who want to take a wacky extended vacation.
   - As executive director, he might not be in a position to approve such a large sum without consulting other officers of the foundation.

7. **STRATEGIES TO BE USED DURING THE VISIT (plans to overcome the possible obstacles)**
   - Use the photos from our Central America trip to impress Mr. Page with the philosophy guiding our concept. Convince him that funding such a singular project will reflect well upon the reputation of the Jerry James Foundation.
   - Use the fact that we paid for the first trip to indicate our commitment and focus. Emphasize that we intend to travel to trouble spots worldwide.
   - Listen carefully to Mr. Page in order to help determine our next step. Respect his ideas and note the names and positions of his colleagues who will be involved the decision-making process.

8. **ACTIONS TO COMPLETE BEFORE THE VISIT**
   - Edit our photos. Choose ten that best demonstrate our ability to raise the spirits of people of all ages and various cultures.
   - Prepare a budget that is realistic, specific, and not excessive.
   - Understand the funding criteria, goals, and rules of the Jerry James Foundation.

9. **AFTER THE VISIT: SUMMARY AND ACTION ITEMS (Have we met our success criteria?)**

Addi arrived for his meeting with Charles Page a few minutes early. He quickly read through his filled-out SPV form, and then put it aside. He was ready.

After he was escorted into Mr. Page's office, he shook hands with a dapper man who looked more like a professor than the head of a major arts foundation.

"I'm Addi Somekh. It's a pleasure to meet you. Thank you for agreeing to see me."

"Not at all. I liked the way you sold your concept in such a precise, easy-to-understand way," Page said, referring to Addi's Quarter-Page Synopsis. "And everyone in the office got a big kick out of your balloon flower. How long have you been working as a balloon artist?"

Addi told the executive director that he had learned the art back in college and had been making money doing it ever since.

"I've always been amazed at how fascinated people of all ages are when they see a balloon piece taking shape," Addi continued. "How relaxed and at ease they seem to become. It has a way of bringing out the kid in all of us, I think."

"I can understand that," Page said. "So tell me about the Inflatable Crown project, Mr. Somekh."

Then Addi made his presentation, using Charlie's photographs to document the success of their five-week test trip around Central America. He went on to detail the projected itinerary, stressing their desire to include time in places ravaged by poverty and hunger - and repeating the project's tag line: "Laughter sounds the same in every language."

"That's our goal, Mr. Page. To prove that laughter *does* sound the same in every language." And on that note, made a balloon flower for Page's wife and balloon rings and necklaces for his two daughters.

The visit had gone even better than Addi had hoped. Mr. Page was clearly enthusiastic about the concept and delighted with the balloon gifts. He assured Addi that he would consult with the other members of the foundation's board: Conor O'Brien and Denise Rosenberg.

"Such a large funding request requires that I do so," he explained.

When Addi arrived home, he filled in the "After the Visit" summary on his SPV. Although the specified success criteria were yet to be met, he noted, there were several positive aspects of the visit, especially Page's keen interest in the project.

Chapter 5

Single-Page Presentation Guidelines
Excite your audience with clarity and interactivity

It had been four days since my meeting with Charles Page, and I had not yet heard back from him. I wasn't panicked because I realized that these kinds of things take time.

I still hadn't satisfied the success criterion spelled out on my SPV form: "To have Charles Page write a check for $100,000 on the spot, or at least have the Inflatable Crown project put on track to receive funding." But even though I hadn't left the meeting with a funding check, I felt that I'd convinced a key decision-maker at the foundation that the project was worthwhile. I also sensed that Charles Page believed that Charlie and I together possessed the right combination of talents and personalities to execute the ambitious project successfully.

On the fifth day after the meeting, Charles Page phoned. "First of all," he said, "I want you to know that your balloon creations made quite a hit with my family. It was interesting to see firsthand the positive effect balloon art can have on people."

"Glad to hear it," I said. And I was, because it's always gratifying to get a rave review!

"Now, as far as the grant is concerned," Mr. Page continued, "I reviewed your information and think it would be appropriate for you and your partner to make a full presentation to the board."

"We'd love to do it," I said. I was thrilled; this was the best news we could have hoped for. Here was our chance to impress the people who could give the official go-ahead for the grant. "I really appreciate the opportunity."

"By the way, this isn't how we usually do things at the foundation, but I think yours is a unique project. If we do fund it, it will not only say a lot about our commitment to the arts but also about our commitment to the human community worldwide. Of course, the final decision is up to the entire board, so come prepared."

"Absolutely," I said. "When would you like us to be there?"

"A week from today. We'll meet in our conference room, so you'll have access to a projector if you need one."

After hanging up, I allowed myself a few minutes to absorb the good news. Obviously, there were no guarantees that the grant was ours, but we'd taken a big step forward, and now we had to prepare for the next one.

When I called Charlie with the news, he wasn't as elated as I was. He didn't share my optimism. Charlie is from New York, and New Yorkers refuse to get excited until a check has actually cleared. "It's a lot easier to make balloons for a guy to bring home to his family," he said, "than it is to convince three people to write us a check for $100,000."

"And the only way to ensure that," I replied, "is to be as prepared as possible. Let's put our heads together and get things going."

"Works for me," Charlie said. "I'll be over right away."

It occurred to me that another "Hike with Sass" might be in order. All his suggestions so far had been right on the money, and I wasn't about to look past a valuable resource at this stage of the game. Dad had made hundreds of presentations in his day, so he obviously would have a clear understanding of the process.

I e-mailed him, outlining where things stood with the Jerry Jones Foundation and suggesting a morning hike with Charlie. He wrote back: "See you bright and early tomorrow."

Charlie met us at the entrance to the park, and soon the three of us were doing what Sass and I had done the last time out: setting a fast pace and keeping conversation to a minimum. I was fine with that. I needed the exercise, and the amount of huffing and puffing I was doing made intelligent conversation almost impossible.

We took a short break halfway into our climb. That's when Dad said, "So your visit with the executive director got you a meeting with the board!"

"Well, we're making progress," I said. "I can't tell you how much I've gotten out of using those Single-Page concepts of yours."

"I second that," Charlie said.

"It's amazing how the pages keep you focused, isn't it?" Dad replied. "You have another meeting next week, right?"

"Yeah, and we were hoping we could talk with you about the best way to prepare for the presentation," I said.

As we started walking again, he said, "You did a good job in your one-on-one visit with Charles Page, so let's compare it to the upcoming presentation to the foundation board."

"This time, Charlie and I will be going in together, and there will be two other people on the foundation's side."

"So that's three personalities you'll be dealing with," Sass said. "Don't discount that. It's extremely important."

"Seems to me we should start by following some of the same guidelines included on the Single-Page Visit form. We have to have success criteria, and we have to have a strategy to achieve them.

And this time, we'll meet with the three people who have the power to green light our grant."

"Or to red light it," Charlie added.

"So we'll need to stand in front of Page and his colleagues and tell them a story, one that will appeal to three different personalities and perspectives and that will be convincing enough for them to prompt them to write us a $100,000 check."

"That's right. So let's talk about the story part of the presentation," Dad suggested. "What would be a good example of elaborate storytelling? Something we all experience frequently."

"Movies and TV," I answered.

"Okay, so let's try to determine what makes you or me or anyone like a movie, and also what seem to be determining factors in TV ratings."

This was an interesting question, and not one I had anticipated. I wondered where Dad was going with this and how it related to our presentation.

Eventually, I said, "I like it when a movie engages me right from the start and keeps my interest from beginning to end. I like a powerful conclusion. And I get a bit bored when a story takes too much time to develop."

"Yes, and what about the clarity of the story?" Dad asked.

"I like an elaborate story, but I also get frustrated when it's *too* complicated, so much so that you feel like you'd have to read the book to grasp what's going on."

"A movie is meant to entertain and inform, not to confuse," was how Charlie put it.

"Exactly," I replied and then added, "I like action movies, but not when the action is excessive. Quality should be more important than quantity."

"What about television, Charlie?" Sass asked. "When compared to movies, what unique characteristics drive TV ratings?"

Charlie didn't hesitate: "It seems to me that programs that incorporate audience feedback have pretty good ratings."

As we continued our hike, we talked about incorporating some of our observations about movies and TV into our presentation. "The point," Sass said, "is that you want to get your audience involved and keep them involved, you want to keep things moving, and you want to emphasize quality over quantity."

"Is there a formula you use?" Charlie asked.

"Not a formula per se, because every presentation is different, but a definitely a set of guidelines," Sass said. "I think you'll find the Single-Page Presentation Guidelines, or SPPG, that I use quite helpful."

"One more thing," he said looking at Charlie. "Good slides are like good photography: both enhance the delivery of your story. That's why I included a section in the SPPG on how to maximize the potential of slides in a presentation."

Single-Page Presentation Guidelines (SPPG)

Preparation

1. Tailor the presentation to the situation. Start with a strategy:
   a. Audience composition.
   b. Success criteria for the presentation.
   c. Problems that could be obstacles to success.
   d. Strategies to overcome the obstacles.
   e. Actions that need to be taken prior to the presentation.
2. Plan to start with "a brick through a glass window." Is there a "wow factor" related to your project, your market, or your team?
3. Structure the presentation with the appropriate outline. For example, for a presentation in which you seek funding for your business, use these outline headings: Introduction, Team, Market, Product, Competition, Strategy, Timeline, Financials and Summary.
4. Frame your message using the Problem/Benefit/Solution/Proof format.
   a. Give a background if required
   b. Describe a key problem/opportunity.
   c. Describe the benefits of solving the problem/pursuing the opportunity.
   d. Describe your solution.
   e. Conclude, if possible, with proof that the solution indeed works.
5. Prepare your slides carefully and follow the 10 "Slides Etiquette Rules" below:
   1. Make the slides self-explanatory – will avoid clarification questions, and allow the presentation to stand by itself, making it easier for an internal champion to promote your cause after the meeting.
   2. Be sure every slide is necessary. Too much information can be distracting.
   3. Use bullet animation to ensure that your audience is not reading ahead; remember however, that excessive animation could be annoying and will slow things down.
   4. Use font sizes that will be readily legible given the size of the presentation room.
   5. Make sure text is legible when placed on a colored background.
   6. Avoid acronyms that may not be familiar to the audience.
   7. Make charts easy to comprehend. Avoid vertical text, distribute legends next to the actual data.
   8. Reserve Green for Good, Red for Bad, and a visible Yellow for Neutral. (Note: Use Color code that is suitable for the region of the globe. For example, Red is Good, not Bad in China)
   9. Start the slide's message with the title. Use "This is better than that" instead of "This vs. that"
   10. Encapsulate the message of the slide in a "takeaway box" at the bottom of the slide.
6. Plan to engage the audience with pictures, videos, props, demos etc.

Delivery:

7. Re-check how much time is allotted for your presentation. If your time is cut substantially, do not try to go through all the material but go to the key slides in order to deliver the key message.
8. Verify the audience's interests, if not done prior to the presentation, by asking if the outline meets their expectations.
9. Deliver with passion and enthusiasm, using natural gestures to make key points and maintaining eye contact with all your listeners (left, right, front, and back).
10. Watch the audience's body language. Solicit feedback, and adjust accordingly.
11. Answer a question after making sure you fully understand it (don't hesitate to ask for clarification), pause to think, and answer sincerely. After answering, verify that the answer was satisfactory. If the answer to a question is covered later in the presentation, give "the short answer," and provide the details in due course. If you encounter strong, justified objection, do not give up. Pause, gather your thoughts, acknowledge the issue but counter it with multiple positive attributes from your side.
12. Conclude, depending on your success criteria, by "asking for the order" or by asking for feedback so you can determine if your success criteria has been met. Then summarize the feedback and the action/follow up items collected during the meeting.

Download at www.TheBalancedManager.com

Charlie and I decided to meet again in order to make the best use of the SPPG and be sure we knew exactly what we wanted to achieve in the forty-five minutes the board had allotted for our meeting.

Preparation

The first thing we did was update the Single-Page Visit form I had used for my initial meeting with Charles Page, including adding two names to our list of participants.

Our research identified Conor O'Brien as a fifty-five-year-old CPA who owned his own firm. A member of the foundation's board for six years, he had graduated from the University of Washington and taught accounting classes pro bono at a community college in San Francisco. It wasn't much, but it told us O'Brien was an entrepreneur with a philanthropic bent.

Denise Rosenberg was forty-one-year-old single mother with a background in investment banking. She has been with Bank of America for the past thirteen years, and was also on the board of directors of the San Francisco Aquarium, so apparently she was as interested in nature as she was in the arts.

While our success criterion remained the same - procuring the necessary grant for our global journey - the problem statement was more complex, given the additional participants. We would now need to consider the entire board's view of balloon art, especially with regard to the endeavor we were proposing. Would they regard it as an art form worthy of their support, or as something frivolous and, combined with the scope of our trip, a project idea fraught with risks? We would also need to consider the interaction among the board members themselves. Was there one with extra influence, or were they all on an equal footing? Finally, were they likely to express independent, similar, or opposite opinions?

Because I would be handling much of the oral presentation while Charlie would be in charge of visuals, I knew I would have to rely on my people-observation skills and my ability to improvise and adapt: observe the board members, process the information, and adjust to the situation. And, of course, trust my instincts while showing absolute confidence in our proposed undertaking.

Charlie and I tailored our presentation according to the SPPG, keeping in mind the material that had worked so well in my meeting with Charles Page. We also spent hours doing a proper photo edit. We wanted to use enough images to show the range of our work and to evoke the kinds of emotion we knew the photos could inspire.

We did two dry runs the day before the meeting and felt good about our strategy.

Delivery

When we entered the room the next morning, the three board members were already seated. I shook Page's hand, and he gave me a supportive smile. One down, two to go, I thought. Then he introduced his fellow board members.

Denise Rosenberg was an attractive woman who looked less like an investment banker than a somewhat bohemian artist from the 1960s. She had a firm handshake and an engaging smile, and my first impression was that she would be relatively easy to win over if the presentation went as planned.

Conor O'Brien, on the other hand, was conservatively dressed and anything but cordial. He seemed a little annoyed at having to stand and shake our hands. Apparently, our entrance had interrupted whatever he was doing on his Blackberry. This one, I thought, is going to be a challenge.

"Why don't you take a moment to set up the projector and arrange your materials," Page said. "Then we'll get started."

When we were ready, I gave a brief introduction and then showed them two slides. The first captured a violent anti-American demonstration in Africa. The second was a *New York Times* headline of an article about a hate crime committed here in San Francisco.

I paused, looked directly at each board member, and asked the two questions that were at the heart of the Inflatable Crown project: "Can art make even the smallest dent in the seemingly endless cycle of bad news? Can art change the perspective of men, women, and children? Our contention is that it can."

Charles Page, of course, knew what was coming, and smiled. Denise Rosenberg nodded sympathetically. Conor O'Brien's face was expressionless.

I reached into my pocket for a half-dozen colored balloons and went to work. I could see Denise smiling as a tall, colorful flower suddenly took shape, and I could sense her delight when I presented it to her. She put a hand over her heart and smiled broadly. "I can see how this would make people happy. And I can see how a balloon crown on a young child's head provokes laughter, too."

Conor O'Brien said nothing, his expression still blank.

After I described the goals we hoped to achieve if we could launch the project, Charlie showed several slides from our Central American trip. "I only wish you could hear the laughter of these people," I said, as Charlie began leading them on a brief photographic journey from Guatemala to Nicaragua, mixing the faces of smiling kids with those of elderly men with wrinkled faces.

"Balloons can be the unique social interaction," I said, continuing the pitch. "Every time I make a balloon hat, I'm basically giving a live performance. The audience sees it happening in front of their eyes. Then they can actually wear the art they've seen created."

Conor O'Brien was still expressionless.

I explained that while the goal of the test-run Central American trip had been to make people laugh and to spark a bit of happiness in them, we were surprised to find that it had also helped one community connect with its past. At that point, Charlie took up the story and told about the small settlement of Mosquito Indians deep in Nicaragua. He showed several photos of laughing kids and smiling adults and ended with an image of one of the community elders. Charlie recalled: "He came up to me and said, 'You don't know how important it is for the children to see these hats and to wear them. These are very similar to the hats our ancestors wore, hats from the feathers of birds that are no longer here.' You can imagine how Addi and I treasure the memory of that encounter."

When I resumed talking, I explained our strategy, timeline, and budget. Our allotted time was drawing to a close, and I needed a strong finish.

Closure

"We intend to go to as many trouble spots in the world as we can," I said fervently, "to demonstrate how even people in the most desperate situations can find joy and camaraderie in something as simple and fun as a hat made from a balloon."

As I ran down our list of intended destinations and came to Northern Ireland, Conor O'Brien finally reacted. He looked up, and I could see the intensity in his eyes, his visceral connection to that conflicted land.

I knew I had to use this moment to get him on board. "We all know that bad news travels a lot faster than good news, I said. "And often people only hear the negative side of the stories from a particular place, especially when it comes to war news. What we want to do is show the happy, positive moments of everyday life, those moments that almost never make the headlines."

I paused and let the words sink in. Conor O'Brien glanced at Denise Rosenberg and nodded.

Chapter 6

Single-Page Strategy
Summarize your strategy with focus and precision

When Addi phoned the day after his presentation to the Jerry James Foundation board, I could tell by the sound of his voice that he had good news to share.

"Charles Page called and said the board was impressed with our presentation. They think the Inflatable Crown project will have positive wide-reaching results, and said they've been waiting to support something with such global appeal. They approved our grant, Dad! That means they'll be cutting us a check for a $100K. Hard to believe, isn't it?'

"Not at all," I said. "You've handled the entire process up to now like a pro, and obviously the foundation thinks so, too. I'm proud of you, Addi. Proud of Charlie, also. Why don't Mom and I take you two out for dinner, and we'll do a little celebrating. You've earned it."

That evening at a local restaurant, it became clear that Addi and Charlie were both thunderstruck by their sudden good fortune. Addi, who's normally upbeat and never at a loss for words, was uncharacteristically quiet.

Eta asked, "So now that you're about to be handed $100,000, how does it feel? You seem a little shell-shocked."

"To tell you the truth," said Addi, "I feel like a puppy that decided to chase the fastest car on the block, actually caught up with the car, and now doesn't quite know what to do."

"I couldn't agree more," Charlie said.

We laughed at the image, but I understood that it captured how overwhelmed both young men felt at the prospect of following through on something that, until now, had just been an idea on paper.

I raised my wine glass and toasted them. "Here's to you both. You should feel proud of this accomplishment. You've been able to create a vision and articulate it in such a way that an established organization with a nationwide reputation is willing to sponsor you."

"Right," said Charlie. "And now we have to go out and execute that vision."

"Exactly. And what do you need in order to execute well?" I asked, looking across the table at Addi.

"Plans are nothing," he smiled, repeating General Eisenhower's famous words. "*Planning* is everything."

"That's right. And you've already proven that," I said. "You generated a plan for your first visit with Mr. Page, and then you planned a successful presentation and pulled it off flawlessly. So the next question is: How will you go about creating a grand strategy for your project, now that you have the funding to proceed?"

"We start with our success criteria, listing all the things we want to accomplish over the course of the project," Addi said.

"Yes. A prioritized list of accomplishments. Know what your most important goals are and focus on those. And then?"

"And then we need to identify the key problems we'll have to overcome to attain those goals," Charlie answered. "Having the funding is just the beginning."

"Basically, we need to create strategies to reach our goals, and an action plan to implement the strategies," Addi said with conviction.

I sat back and watched them take charge of the idea, two partners effectively complementing each other - Addi the conceptual guy and Charlie the detail-oriented perfectionist.

As the conversation continued, Addi and Charlie mentioned some of the places they intended to visit. "The idea is to show that a village in Brazil is not so different from a town in the States," Addi told us. "We're all human beings, right? We're all striving to feed our families and to keep a roof over our heads. We all face problems. We all experience successes and failures. And we all love to laugh."

"I like your slogan," Eta said. "'Laughter sounds the same in every language.' It's true. Laughter really is one of the things that bind us all together."

"And proving that is one of our goals," Addi said. "Now that we have the resources to move forward, we have to treat this project like we would any start-up business. After all, what we're doing is not all so different from opening a restaurant or launching a software company. One outcome of our travels has to be a product or products that people will appreciate and be willing to buy. Whether it's a calendar or a book or something we haven't thought of yet, it has to be commercially viable."

"You should summarize your strategy on a single page," I advised.

"I'll do it as soon as we get home," Addi promised. "But enough about business for now. Let's eat."

We followed Addi's lead and instead discussed the cultural differences he and Charlie would encounter in the various countries they soon would visit. It became clear that preparing for and dealing with these differences would be just one of many challenges they would face over the next few years.

It was apparent - and gratifying - to me that Addi and Charlie were viewing their trip not only as an art project but also as a business venture, an undertaking with concrete goals and the need for a sound strategy.

As he said he would, Addi promptly completed an SPS - Single-Page Strategy form. After reviewing it, I handed him a remarkably similar page from a product-development project I had previously overseen. I wanted him to see the Single-Page concept from a different perspective - in this case, the development of the Precision 5000, a system used in computer-chip production.

I chose an SPS related to a project that was very different from the Inflatable Crown. My rationale was to demonstrate to Addi and Charlie that the Single-Page approach was broadly applicable. If you know your goals and know the challenges involved in achieving them, and if you develop a plan and execute it, then you are likely to succeed. In fact, the Precision 5000 system was so technically revolutionary and such a commercial success that it was displayed at the American History Museum of the Smithsonian Institution in Washington, D.C.

Addi studied the Single-Page Strategy for the Precision 5000 and then completed the SPS for the Inflatable Crown. Here's how the two compare.

Single-Page Strategy (SPS)
The Precision 5000 System   Jan. 13, 1986

1. **BACKGROUND (facts, figures, and key assumptions)**

   The computer-chip industry is a $30B/year business, growing rapidly at the rate of 16%/year. Chip makers buy $6B/year worth of manufacturing equipment, an amount projected to double in five years.

   The two leading equipment market segments are Etch and CVD (Chemical Vapor Deposition). The equipment industry is fragmented; it lacks a strong leader, and has no companies that lead in more than one segment.

2. **SUCCESS CRITERIA (measurable and scheduled key results)**

   a. Within five years, become the leader in Etch and CVD, with a market share of at least 30% in each area.

   b. Achieve a high level of customer satisfaction (90% in customer surveys).

   c. Ensure a profitable business with gross margin greater than 60%.

3. **PROBLEM STATEMENT (obstacles to success)**

   a. We only have an aging Etch product and no CVD product.

   b. Due to the recession this year, the company does not have enough funds to develop a new product, let alone two products simultaneously.

   c. Previously developed products were technologically successful but suffered from low customer satisfaction due to poor equipment reliability.

   d. Previously developed products only became highly profitable two years after being introduced on the market.

4. **STRATEGIES (plans to resolve obstacles)**

   a. Leverage our newly invented concept of a "multi-chamber system." Instead of developing two systems (Etch and CVD), develop a single system with CVD and Etch chambers at a substantial savings.

   b. Secure funds for product development by engaging a key customer willing to invest in the company for an early access to the Etch and CVD products.

   c. Emphasize equipment reliability during product development:
      - Leverage Japanese reliability reputation by recruiting some engineers from Japan.
      - Assemble an independent reliability-verification team.

   d. Assemble a "concurrent manufacturing" team that will continuously analyze cost and profitability during the design phase.

5. **DELIVERABLES OVER THE NEXT TWELVE MONTHS (item, date, owner)**

   a. Reach investment agreement with key customer by 3/31/86 (division vice president)

   b. Assemble all teams by 4/30/86 (department heads)

   c. Finalize system, Etch and CVD chambers concepts by 9/30/86 (project manager)

   d. Ship first CVD system to a key customer by 3/31/87 (project manager)

Download at www.TheBalancedManager.com

Single-Page Strategy (SPS)
The Inflatable Crown April 12

1. **BACKGROUND (facts, figures, and key assumptions):**

   a. The Jerry James foundation has granted Addi and Charlie $100,000 to carry out their vision of a social experiment called The Inflatable Crown: Laughter Sounds the Same in Every Language.

   b. The grant underwrites trips to a few dozen countries. It does not fund the publication of a book documenting the project, the creation or distribution of a related wall calendar, or the production of a video.

2. **SUCCESS CRITERIA (measurable and scheduled key results)**

   a. To entertain, educate, and inspire people by proving that laughter sounds the same in every language.

   b. To produce a photography book and wall calendar as well as a movie and a website within three years.

   c. To realize a profit by marketing the book, calendar, and the movie without compromising the project's integrity.

   d. To use the overall experience as a foundation for career development.

3. **PROBLEM STATEMENT (obstacles to success):**

   a. Addi and Charlie are a good team in terms of the balloon art, photography, and writing aspects of the project, but neither has experience in film/video work, publishing, or Web design.

4. **STRATEGIES (plans to resolve the obstacles):**

   a. Locate and recruit a documentary filmmaker to become a part of the Inflatable Crown project.

   b. Find and work with a person knowledgeable about the process of book publishing.

   c. Learn how to design a Web site that will effectively publicize the project.

5. **DELIVERABLES OVER THE NEXT TWELVE MONTHS (item, date, owner)**

   a. Recruit a reputable videographer within three months (Charlie).

   b. Plan logistics for the first leg of the trip (Europe) within three months (Addi).

   c. Create a maximum budget of $15,000 for the first leg of the trip (Addi and Charlie).

   d. Recruit a reputable Webmaster to assist in building a superior Web site within eight months (Addi).

   e. Plan the next leg of the trip and depart in nine months (Charlie).

Addi felt he had accomplished an essential task after completing the Single-Page Strategy form. He also realized that he would be updating the SPS on a regular basis as circumstances dictate and plans evolve. He sent a copy to Charlie, and the two of them discussed it in detail, making a few minor adjustments to their written plan of action.

Now they would devote their energies to turning the tasks listed in number five on the form into tangible results. The next day, Addi began the paperwork to establish The Inflatable Crown LLC, of which he and Charlie were the partners. He also opened a checking account; as soon as they heard from the foundation, he would arrange a wire transfer of the money. Before long, the project would be officially up and running.

Chapter 7

Single-Page Report
Report news - good, bad, or indifferent - in order of importance

The next morning, I received a call from Raymond Clister, chief financial officer of the Jerry James Foundation. By this time, I had informed the foundation's accounting office about our bank account for the Inflatable Crown and also had forwarded the necessary wiring instructions.

"Mr. Somekh," he said, "I want to let you know that $100,000 has been wired to your account at First National Bank of San Francisco. Congratulations."

"Thank you. We're looking forward to getting started," I replied - an understatement if ever there was one.

"I will be e-mailing confirmation from our end shortly, and you should receive notification from your bank this morning, too," he said. "I also want to let you know that the foundation requires a monthly report so we can track the progress of your project."

"I wasn't aware of that," I said, although it certainly was a reasonable requirement. After all, the foundation had just given us a sizable sum, and so it certainly had the right to track how we were using it.

Later that day, Charlie and I reconvened. Plans for our first trip were in full swing. We had found a videographer named Andy Vermouth to accompany us on our trips, and now we had the money to book our flights and confirm our travel arrangements. I opened with the news of our fully funded bank account, gave Charlie a high five, and then told him we'd be required to submit a monthly report to the foundation.

"I knew it was too good to be true," Charlie grumbled. "The foundation is enthusiastic enough about our project to hand us an exceptionally generous grant, and then they turn around and demonstrate they're not much different than any other bureaucratic organization. Besides, don't they know we're going to be living out of a suitcase for the next couple of years?"

"Well, it's up to you to deal with this, since you're going to be handling most of the paperwork." Charlie was the organized partner, and he already had made our travel and living arrangements.

"I wonder if it makes sense to call the guy back and try to convince him that we'd make better use of their money if we could focus on our work instead of writing reports," Charlie said.

"Let's think about this first," I suggested. "I've seen my dad grapple with plenty of professional problems just by sitting down with a pen and paper and balancing the pros and cons of taking action. Let's give it a try."

"I'm game," Charlie said with a shrug. "He hasn't steered us wrong yet."

I created two columns on a clean piece of paper: "Reasons against doing the monthly report," and "Reasons for doing the monthly report." Then we started brainstorming.

<u>Reasons against doing the report:</u>

Will consume a significant amount of time.

<u>Reasons for doing the report:</u>

Will force us to check how we are doing against our original plan.

Will force us to plan ahead in a systematic way.

Will facilitate communication among our team members.

Will facilitate communication with our sponsor.

Will allow us to demonstrate our successes to the sponsor. (This will be useful should we need additional funds.)

Charlie smiled and conceded, "Well, I think we can skip that phone call, don't you?"

"No doubt about it," I said.

"But what format are we going to use for our monthly report?" Charlie said.

"As you said, my dad hasn't steered us wrong yet. Let's see if he can help us," I said.

Later, Sass joined us, and Charlie told him about my conversation with Raymond Clister. Since we're required to submit monthly reports of our activities, we wonder if you might have an appropriate form we could use for writing periodic reports."

"As a matter of fact, I do," Dad said. "It's called the Single-Page Report, or SPR, and was helpful during the development phase of the Precision 5000. It's simple, direct, and provides a timely snapshot of the project's status."

Single-Page Report (SPR)
Precision 5000 Monthly Report Oct. 31, 1986

Executive Summary

We have finalized the concepts for the system and its chambers one month behind schedule. Customer is enthusiastic about the technical results, but problems persist with the high-temperature parts in the CVD chamber.

Key Accomplishments/problems in order of importance (☺☹☺):

☺ We have finalized and "frozen" the design aspect of our Etch and CVD product - main system and both chambers. This allows us now to do a final design, supplier selection, and preparation for manufacturing. Although completed a month behind the original schedule, we can compress the remaining period and ship the first customer system on schedule five months from now.

☺ We have demonstrated to our key customer and investor the technical capability of the two products, and customer reaction was positive regarding the technical performance of the products. We have met the technical-performance criteria specified in the investment agreement with the customer, who is now waiting for our first system delivery on March 31, 1987.

☹ Reliability: We have lingering problems with failure of parts in the CVD chamber. The parts must operate at high temperatures and are exposed to corrosive gases. The reliability team has identified it as the key remaining issue, and the design team is working on a protective coating. We expect to get samples and test next month.

Plans for next period, in order of importance

1. Receive samples and qualify new coating for parts in CVD chamber.
2. Final design of system and chambers with finite element analysis.
3. Release parts drawings of system and CVD chambers to suppliers.

Key Milestones (prior dates, current date, milestone)

1. ~~9/30/86~~ 10/31/86: Finalize system, Etch, and CVD chambers concepts.
2. ~~10/31/86~~ 11/30/86: Release drawings to suppliers.
3. ~~1/2/87~~ 1/15/87: Begin assembly of first two systems.
4. 3/31/87: Ship first CVD system to key customer.

Key Financial Data (in the organization's common format)

1. Research and development spending: on budget
2. System-material cost: 5% above target

Attachments (Optional reading only):

Customer technical demonstration report.

Download at www.TheBalancedManager.com

Chapter 8

Single-Page Negotiation
Negotiate effectively and build a positive relationship

Over the course of the next few years Charlie, Andy, and I traveled to 34 countries to prove our contention that "laugher sounds the same in every language." My balloon art struck a positive chord everywhere we went. People found it fun and fascinating, playful and meaningful. We brought joy to kids in Bosnia and Northern Ireland, to field workers in India and in Vietnam, to mothers and fathers in Israel and Palestine. Laughter, no matter where we heard it or under what circumstances, seemed to bring out the best in people and unite them in a gratifying way. Overall, the experience showed us a joyful side of human-kind quite different from what we see in the news every day.

Charlie and I truly believed we had achieved a key aspect of our Success Criteria. And the response of the Jerry James Foundation to the photographs Charlie shot and the video footage Andy produced clearly indicated how pleased our donors were as well.

Once we returned home, we began work on the next stages of the project. While Andy edited his documentary movie, Charlie and I signed a book deal with a major publishing house who committed to a first printing of 50,000 copies. We also reached an agreement in principle with Major League Productions (MLP) for the creation and distribution of an Inflatable Crown wall calendar. But even though both sides seemed excited by the commercial viability of the calendar, the deal hit a major snag involving ownership rights, photo selection, and payments.

Unfortunately, we couldn't resolve any of these issues during our first face-to-face meeting with MLP. I anticipated that both sides would have to compromise and that some delicate negotiations would be involved.

What came to mind as I began thinking up a strategy was, interestingly, an antiques swap meet I had gone to with Sass some years earlier. An avid collector of antique radios, Sass was always on the lookout for additions to his collection, and he had developed a discerning eye for the most unusual and authentic pieces. Every year, he went to at least one swap meet sponsored by the California Historical Radio Society, and one time, I accompanied him.

When we arrived, the parking lot was jammed with booths and stands, packed with hundreds of vintage radios. As we strolled from one stand to another, Sass spotted a classic 1921 RCA radio in a beautiful wood cabinet handcrafted in the shape of a clock. It was priced at $300, which Sass felt was too expensive. He offered $150 to the seller, who promptly rejected it. Sass then suggested we shop around and look for "comparables, just like a real estate appraiser would do," he said.

So we stopped at a couple of booths and a half dozen stands with radios similar in vintage to the RCA, talked to the vendors, and learned that their prices were all around $200. When we returned for another look at the RCA model, Sass asked the seller why his radio was more expensive than the competition.

"Because of the radio tubes," the man answered. "It has an original set of almost-new 01A tubes."

When the seller turned his attention to another potential customer, Dad explained that he was really more interested in the radio's unique cabinet than in its tubes.

"I've got a bunch of tubes at home that will work as well as the 01As in this radio," he told me.

The seller returned and asked, "So, what do you think?"

"I'm wondering if you would consider selling the radio without the tubes," Sass proposed.

The seller didn't hesitate. "Sure. Without the tubes, you can have it for $150."

"Done," Sass said, agreeing to a deal both men felt good about. He opened his wallet and paid in cash.

In retrospect, I realized I had witnessed the kind of negotiation that left both parties happy. There had been no "winner" and no "loser." Both parties profited, and I learned a valuable lesson, one I thought I could use now in bridging the gap in our stalled negotiations with Major League Productions. If there was a single- page approach to developing strategy, planning a presentation, or creating a monthly report, surely there should be a Single-Page Negotiation. In this case, the single page could be a blackboard on which all the parties involved could see the progress being made and participate openly in the process.

Charlie and I decided to propose that approach during our next meeting. The owner, Ryan Martin, was only slightly older than we were and had been in business for nearly three years. MLP was a small operation, but one with a growing reputation. I had felt comfortable with Ryan from the beginning of our discussions about the calendar, and I was confident he wanted to find an equitable solution as much as we did. The three of us met in a small conference room, and I was glad to see it contained a blackboard.

I volunteered to be the facilitator of the negotiating session. I began by drawing a horizontal line at the top of the blackboard and dividing the space below into three columns.

"In terms of our collaboration, how would each of you define success?" I asked.

"That's easy," Ryan responded. "Bottom line, I want the calendar to make money." Charlie readily agreed.

In the center column I wrote, "Producing a profitable calendar."

"And the success of the calendar will also allow me to expand our business to include such items as greeting cards and other accessories," Ryan added.

"And for Addi and me," Charlie replied, "a successful calendar will help us promote our book."

In the center column, I listed the key phrases I'd just heard:

- Producing a profitable calendar
- Launching a line of accessory items for MLP
- Publishing a successful Inflatable Crown book

I combined those phrases into a single statement, which I wrote at the top of the board, above the horizontal line: "Success criteria: Profitable calendar, followed by accessory items for MLP and a successful Inflatable Crown book."

I erased the list in the center column.

I then asked Ryan and Charlie to tell me all the obstacles they anticipated to achieving the success criteria.

"First of all," Ryan said, "MLP has to be the owner of all photographs used in the calendar and any accessory items."

I jotted this down in the center column.

"There's no way I can give up ownership of the pictures," Charlie snapped. I reminded him that at that point we were only collecting issues and that we would discuss the issues only after we had listed all of them.

"And I have to have control over which picture we choose for the calendar's cover," Ryan added.

"The problem is that the picture Ryan has chosen for the cover is not acceptable . . ."

"No discussion yet," I reminded Charlie.

"Okay," Charlie said. "My problem is that I need $1,000 for production costs up front."

"Anything else?" I asked. They both shook their heads, so I quickly summarized the issues in the left-hand column and then erased my notes from the center column.

Issues
- Photo ownership
- Cover picture
- $1,000 production payment in advance

At this point, it seemed that the easiest problem to resolve might be the cover picture. I wrote "Cover Picture" at the top of the center column, and said to Ryan, "So, looking at the cover photo, what is the reason or root cause for your choice?"

"If the calendar is to be successful, the cover should appeal to all types of buyers - young and old, male and female," he said. I summarized his input in the center column. Then he pointed to a photo of a Guatemalan family standing next to their grain field, all wearing multicolored balloon hats and broad smiles. "In my opinion, this photo does just that."

"I want the calendar to be successful, too," Charlie said emphatically. "But from an artistic point of view, this picture is one of my least favorites. We have to do better,"

"In that case," I suggested, "why don't you two sit down with Charlie's picture database and look for an image that satisfies both of you."

Charlie agreed and opened his portfolio. He and Ryan started reviewing the pictures, discussing each in turn and why one worked and another didn't. After about half an hour and 200 pictures, they agreed on the cover image: a young girl in Joshua Tree, California, with a bright smile and a wonderfully colorful inflatable crown. In this respect, at least, the negotiation process worked well.

I wrote the selected picture number in the right-hand column under "Solutions." Then I erased the phrases in the center column and wrote down the next problem we needed to tackle: the $1,000 advance for production costs.

Once again, I asked Charlie and Ryan to articulate their positions.

Charlie explained: "I need the money to produce the proofs required for the calendar. Our grant doesn't cover such costs, and I don't have that kind of money myself."

"I understand that," Ryan replied, "but we operate on a tight budget, and it's company policy that the artist is responsible for providing the proofs."

After they had gone back and forth for a while without a resolution, I spoke up. "We need to do some brainstorming here, guys, and come up with a few creative solutions. What if MLP gives Charlie a $1,000 advance and then deducts it from his royalties?"

"Or," Charlie said brightly, "what if we use a digital format for the proofs? That would be half the cost."

"But what about the quality?" Ryan asked.

"It won't reduce the quality at all."

"Alright then," Ryan said. "We'll use the digital format, and MLP will advance Charlie $500 to do the proofs."

"Agreed," Charlie said.

"Good solution," I said, noting it on the right side of the blackboard. We had solved two of our three problems, and the level of cooperation was impressive.

I once again cleared the center column and wrote down the last and toughest problem to be resolved: Photo ownership.

Once more, I asked for the root cause of their positions.

Ryan didn't hesitate. "We have to own the photographs because if the calendar is successful, we'll need them in order to develop a card line and to create other accessories. Otherwise, the arrangement doesn't make any sense or fulfill my success criteria."

"The same argument applies to me," Charlie said. "I have to retain ownership of the pictures because I'm going to need them for the book as well as for spin-offs, such as the documentary, the exhibitions and competitions I want to participate in."

Fortunately, the tendency toward cooperation that had served Charlie and Ryan well in resolving the first two obstacles enabled them to reach a mutually agreeable solution. Charlie would retain ownership of all pictures, and MLP would, in return, have the exclusive right to use a set of these pictures for calendars, greeting cards, and other related items that might follow the successful launch of the calendar. I added the third solution to the right side of the board and erased the center column.

"That went really well," Ryan said. "What's the story with the negotiating process you used?"

"It's called the Single-Page Negotiation."

"Can you send me a copy?"

"I'd be happy to," I said, and the next day, I sent the SPN to Ryan at Major League Productions.

Single-Page Negotiation (SPN)

1. This technique helps bridge a gap between the differing positions of parties interested in reaching an agreement. It works well with a neutral facilitator, but a person from either party could facilitate instead.

2. Start by drawing the simple chart below on a large blackboard or other such similar space.

3. Ask both sides to describe what each would consider a successful outcome. Solicit input from each participant, and write these in the center section of the chart. Allow participants to ask clarification questions but not to engage in discussion. After collecting all input, start a discussion to prioritize the points made and combines them into common success criteria. Write these at the top of the board.

4. Ask participants to name all issues, concerns, and questions that must be resolved in order to reach an agreement that fulfills the success criteria. Allow clarification questions, but avoid discussion as of yet. List the issues raised in the center column of the chart. Re-write the issues on the left side of the chart while grouping together similar points.

5. Pick an easy issue first. Reaching a resolution on the first issue will foster a sense of cooperation in working together to find solutions.

6. Use the following process:
   a. List the issue in the center column on the board.
   b. Write down each side's position.
   c. Ensure that the positions are reasonable by looking at "comparables" adjusted for the situation under consideration.
   d. Get each party to explain the "root cause" of its insistence on its position.
   e. Try to collect at least three ways to address the root causes; challenge both sides to come up with creative ideas.
   f. Always seek a creative idea where neither side "wins" or "loses," but where all root causes are addressed and both sides are satisfied.
   g. If you are unable to resolve a particular issue, set it aside and continue with the others. It may be easier to solve later, as the group may develop a greater level of mutual trust and then be willing to compromise more. In addition, once you have touched on all the issues, it might be possible to offer a compromise that will include give-and-take on certain issues.
   h. If you reach a dead-end or if emotions flare, take a time-out to allow relaxation, re-consideration and possibly behind-the-scene mediation.
   i. Once a solution is reached, write it on the right side of the board.

7. Once the group has resolved all the issues, you might want to suggest to everyone to "sleep on it," so the parties can either come back with a re-enforced commitment to the agreement, or reopen specific issues for further discussion.

Success criteria:

Issues/concerns/questions:		Solutions:

Download at www.TheBalancedManager.com

Chapter 9

Single-Page Action
Explore root causes, define solutions, and drive actions

I remember first learning about the concept of "root cause" during a family trip to Japan, right after I'd graduated from high school. At that time, the Japanese economy was burgeoning. Dad's company was one of the largest American exporters of high-tech equipment to Japan. Sass would travel there at least once a month, and he developed a great appreciation for the country's "quality culture." That's why he planned for my brother and me to visit a high school in Tokyo and a manufacturing plant in Toyota City. He wanted us to understand the Japanese dedication to quality.

Dad used two terms when describing his observations of the quality culture in Japan: *kaizen* and "root cause."

The word *kaizen* basically means continuous improvement - in other words, a constant striving toward perfection. One might say that it is the antithesis of the expression – "If it ain't broke, don't fix it."

"Root-cause" refers to the Japanese practice of seeking and resolving the *basis* of a problem instead of just mitigating its symptoms.

I also remember how Sass compared Japan with the United States.

"If the quality culture is Japan's strength," he explained, "innovation is the key advantage of the United States." With this innovation advantage in mind, he always insisted on having at least three different solutions for any problem he and his company faced at any given time.

I kept these fundamentals in mind as Charlie and I proceeded with the Inflatable Crown book deal and with production of the Inflatable Crown wall calendar. For the most part, the book project was on track: the publisher ordered an initial printing of 50,000 copies to be released in the spring. We were ahead of schedule in presenting the publisher with the photographs and text to be included in the book, and a designer was working on the layout.

The calendar, however, was another story. As the deadline for submitting it to the printer approached, it became clear that we were facing major delays and that the product might not be ready in time for the pre-winter-holidays calendar season. Any wall calendar that hit stores any later than November 1st had little chance of garnering the sales numbers Charlie and I were projecting.

This was unacceptable, of course, and I was determined to correct the situation. Recalling the lessons from my visit to Japan, I knew that the solution would involve "root causes" of the difficulty. I approached the situation determined to implement Sass's conviction that there are three solutions to every problem.

My plan was to send Charlie over to the MLP offices to work hand-in-hand with Ryan and his staff to address the problem. Before he left, I gave him the appropriate single-page form - in this case the Single-Page Action, or SPA.

Single-Page Action (SPA)
[Problem Name]   Date:

1. **BACKGROUND:**

2) **SUCCESS CRITERIA** (Measurable and scheduled key results)

3) **PROBLEM STATEMENT** (The problems to be solved)

4) **ROOT CAUSES OF THE PROBLEMS** (due to materials, machines, manpower, methods, measurements and environment)
   a. Collect ideas for possible root causes; allow clarification questions.
   b. Discuss and prioritize possible root causes. Explore the root cause of the root cause; go as deep as needed, as in the following example:
      I)   The car won't start – why?
      II)   The battery is dead – why?
      III)   The alternator isn't working – why?
      IV)   The belt is broken – why?
      V)   Routine servicing wasn't done on time – why?
   c. Plot the root causes, if required, using a tree diagram.

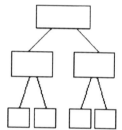

5. **SOLUTIONS FOR THE ROOT CAUSE** (collect 3 ideas, discuss and prioritize):

6. **ACTION ITEMS** (Action, date, owner)

7. **MONITOR PROGRESS** (Create chart, monitor until problems are solved)

Download at www.TheBalancedManager.com

When Charlie felt he had a firm grasp of the SPA approach, he made an appointment to meet with Ryan and two members of Ryan's staff. Rachel was in charge of operations, and Susan handled logistics between Major League Productions and its main suppliers.

Charlie sensed right away that Ryan and his team were as worried about the Inflatable Crown calendar's production as we were. With that in mind, Charlie began the meeting by reaffirming the project's success criteria. "I think everyone agrees that our goal is to publish a successful calendar in time for the calendar sales season."

"Absolutely," Ryan said. "That's the only way we're going to make any money on this deal."

"I agree," Charlie said. "So can I ask everyone to help put together a list of problems that might keep us from achieving the success criteria?"

Rachel spoke first. "Unfortunately, our printer is in China, and we're having a terrible time getting a response to our attempts at communications. This is really putting the schedule at risk."

"And even if we can get the printing back on schedule, there's a longshoremen's strike in San Francisco," Susan said. "This might mean the calendars will get stuck in port even if they do arrive on time, and we'll miss the sales season altogether."

Charlie realized those were two very serious but separate issues.

"Let's start brainstorming the root causes of our difficulty with the Chinese printer," he suggested. Then he wrote down the following:

- The printer in China is not responding. Why?
- MLP has yet to pay its last bill. Why?
- MLP is disputing the charge. Why?
- The printed material MLP received did not look good. Why?
- The printer apparently did not understand MLP's specifications. Why?
- MLP's specs could be interpreted in two ways, and the printer inadvertently picked the "wrong" one.

Next, Charlie encouraged the team to come up with three different solutions for the problem.

"We could look for another printer, either here or in China," suggested Susan.

"We could also forget our billing dispute and get current on our accounts by paying our outstanding bill as is," Rachel offered.

"I could call the printer in China," Ryan said, "and negotiate a settlement to the dispute and get our payment made. I think they know that both sides are responsible for the problem, so we should be able to work it out. I know for sure we couldn't get a new printer up to speed fast enough, even if we could find one here."

The group agreed that Ryan's solution was the best. Charlie noted an action item: Ryan was to resolve the accounts-payable problem, while correcting the specification ambiguity.

"Now, what about our second problem - the longshoremen's strike?" Charlie asked. "I think we can agree that whatever the root cause of the strike is, we're not going to solve it. So let's look at ways we can minimize the damage to our schedule. Any ideas?"

Rachel said, "We could air-ship the calendars, but that wouldn't be cheap."

"Despite the strike, I guarantee our customs agent can do wonders with high-priority shipments," Susan said.

"We can try shipping to another location, but the strike is rumored to be spreading to more ports," added Ryan.

Ultimately, the team members decided that air-shipping the entire order of 10,000 calendars would be too expensive, but if they air- shipped even 1,000 calendars, they would be able to secure shelf space in selected retail outlets.

Rachel offered to handle those arrangements and Charlie said he would contact the customs agent. It was essential she knew what to look for when the shipment finally arrived at the port and so she could assign the calendars high priority.

Reviewing the SPA, Ryan said, "Let's make sure we have our action items in place."

- Ryan to call China immediately, resolve the current issue, and make sure that future specs are written so that they are clear.
- Charlie to visit the customs agent and explain that the calendar shipment requires a high priority.
- Rachel to arrange air-shipment of 1,000 calendars ASAP.

Within a week, Ryan's negotiations regarding the delinquent bill had been successfully concluded, and Susan arranged for a payment. Ryan has also clarified the specs with the printing manager at the Chinese plant.

In early October, a thousand calendars arrived and were promptly distributed to retail outlets around the country. The remaining nine thousand calendars arrived three weeks later and were rushed out the door.

Chapter 10

Practical Relationship-Skills
Experience the art of making people happier

When our calendars appeared in stores on schedule and I saw the positive reactions of people thumbing through them, I felt it finally was time to celebrate. And we had plenty to celebrate: the amazing effort we had put in over the last few years, the remarkable success of our worldwide adventures, the incredible friendships we had developed around the world, and most important, the countless ways we had witnessed how laughter does indeed sound the same in all languages.

One evening, as I was planning our long-overdue celebration, Sass joined me and said,

"I haven't really had a chance to tell you how proud I am of the way you handled yourself ever since we first talked about the Inflatable Crown project. You really tackled it head-on and made it work," he said.

"Thanks, Dad. I appreciate that," I replied. "You know, I couldn't have done it without your help."

"I guess now the $100,000 question is: "Do you think the project met its success criteria?"

It certainly was a question worth asking, and from a business point of view, the only one that really mattered.

Our initial success criteria were:

- To entertain, educate, and inspire people by proving that laughter sounds the same in every language.
- To produce a photography book and wall calendar as well as a movie and a Web site within three years.
- To realize a profit by marketing the book, calendar, and movie without compromising the project's integrity.
- To use the overall experience as a foundation for career development.

"I feel we achieved most of our criteria. We definitely entertained, educated, and inspired people throughout the world. After that, we published a book that's selling really well, and the sales of our calendar are great, too. We created a Web site and a full-length documentary about the project. Although it's too soon to tell if all aspects of the Inflatable Crown project will be financially rewarding, I feel that Charlie and I created good foundations for our career development."

In fact, the twelve thousand outstanding photos Charlie returned home with had given him the confidence to launch his career as a photojournalist. As for me, I had capitalized on my natural ability to make people happier - people representing a range of cultures, countries, languages, religions, and ages. This particular strength not only gave me personal satisfaction but also was in sync with the ideal jobs I had listed for myself on the Single-Page Personal Plan: educator, entertainer, or TV personality.

"Good for you, Addi - and for Charlie as well," Sass said. "Now I have a favor to ask. I'd like you to summarize all these relationship building experiences and thoughts about making people happier, so I can share them with people at work – I believe that job satisfaction is greatly enhanced, for both manager and employee, when the manager possesses good interpersonal and relationship skills."

Here is what I offered Sass several days later.

After all our travels around the world making balloon hats for people, I feel strongly that the happiest a person can be is when he brings happiness to others. It starts with the giver. When the giver reaches out, the happiness bounces off the receiver and goes back to the giver, thus making both people happy.

People are born with certain attributes and talents. And the opposite is also true: other people are born without certain characteristics. For example, one person may be gifted in math while another may have an unusually keen sense of humor. Not everyone can be good at everything.

But we still need to have some proficiency in whatever it is we are not great at, and might even dread doing. The artist still needs to know enough math to balance his check book while the scientist still needs to be personable enough to interact with people at a dinner party. And of course, the manager needs to be proficient in many avenues in life.

Thus, not everyone wants to or is able to be an extroverted entertainer. Yet, there are certain habits or principles that help lubricate social life and make it easier to function with people, whether they are family, colleagues, competitors, or strangers.

We can all learn much about life by simply watching a surfboarder riding an ocean wave. The wave is much bigger and more powerful than the surfer. To stay on top, the surfer has to be alert and responsive, making hundreds of little movements every moment. But at the same time, he has to do the opposite as well: he must relax his control and feel the wave. If he is either too tight or too loose he will fall.

The same is true with social life, which, like a wave, is much bigger than we are as individuals, and we can either get on top of the "wave" or be "pummeled" by it. The secret is to find the balance, the union of opposing forces, so we don't get stuck in one mode of behavior all the time, and so we can be aware and switch to the correct way of dealing with any given situation. Just like learning to surf, it can be tricky at first, with lots of falling. Yet with enough practice and thoughtfulness, anyone can learn to spread joy. And spreading joy is a million times more enjoyable than getting smashed against the rocks.

Below are ten practical interpersonal skills I found most useful during my trips throughout the world. No one needs to be a master of them all, but everyone can make them a part of their lives, both personal and professional.

Addi's 10 Practical Relationship-Skills

1. Make People Feel Important

Have you ever met someone who takes pride in being shallow? Everyone wants to feel their life has meaning and importance – that he or she is the star of the show.

It is just as easy to make someone feel important than it is to make them feel unimportant. Sometimes something as simple as the right choice of words, simply acknowledging someone's work and time makes them feel respected and appreciated, which in turn opens up a reservoir of energy and cooperation. But words can only go so far – often times it may be something much more concrete (a bonus or a promotion) that is required to make a person feel important.

If the opposite happens, and a person feels disrespected, either by accident or on purpose, he or she will close down and carry a load of resentment that only gets heavier and darker.

2. Remember Names

There is an old saying that everyone loves the sound of his or her own name. Hearing the sound of their own name makes them feel important and recognized. By going out of your way to remember someone's name and mentioning it, it makes a subtle, but huge, impression. The difference between, "How are you?" and "Rebecca, how are you today?" is only two words but makes a world of difference.

3. Be Generous but Genuine

But in reality, is everyone really important? Well, that is debatable. But what is not debatable is that your life is easier if the people around you feel you respect them, so it is in your best interest to make them feel that way. At the same time, spraying contrived compliments in all directions won't work either because people will see that as phony.

The answer is to be generous with you compliments, but keep it genuine so it is real and effective. Look for the unique positive attributes of a person and avoid generic platitudes.

For those who feel that social interactions are not their forte, this can feel like an impossible ballet. But in reality there are some very simple first steps.

4. Ask Questions

Often social interactions can be awkward and strange, especially in the workplace where, outside of the task at hand, it can be hard to find common ground to talk to people. One simple way to "lubricate the machinery" is to ask a question. People love to talk about themselves and they love even more to talk about what they love. If you notice something about a person – a photo of their children or a logo of a bowling league, you can simply ask about it. "How many children do you have?" Or "How long have you been bowling?" Usually people will be happy to start talking about their favorite topics. Ask a follow up question and all of a sudden a conversation begins to grow.

Just like riding the wave, the conversation begins to flow in a certain direction and you flow with it. Even if it isn't terribly interesting to you, you are learning something new and showing the person that you respect them enough to know what is important to them. And, without respect, the relationship will not progress much further.

5. Actually Listen

Just like being ignored is annoying and insulting, the opposite is also true – Being heard and acknowledged is one of the positive feelings we receive from society. Having a conversation with someone and not listening is like filling water in a bucket with a hole in it. Empathy, the ability to identify with other people's feelings, is one of the most important talents a manager can have, and it all begins with listening.

In a brainstorming session, the collective wisdom that builds on each other's ideas is usually greater than any one individual's contribution. So, particularly if you are the facilitator, make sure to bring out the collective wisdom by listening intently, striving to understand other people's ideas, and helping the quiet voices be heard as well.

6. Observe Body Language

Words are only one way to express thoughts and feelings. Tone and body language are two other important elements of communication. "I love you forever" sounds bold and powerful, but if the person says it mumbling and slouched over, it means something entirely different. By understanding how someone says something we can reach a deeper understanding of what they really mean. Things like eye contact, body positioning and hand gestures may be even more important than the actual words spoken.

Body language is a field that has been well-researched and familiarizing yourself with the basic principles can help you stay on top of the wave of social interactions.

7. Be Flexible, but not a Pushover

The ultimate trick to stay on the wave is being flexible and firm at the same time. Ironically, parents often say it is the same trick to raising kids. Too much structure is not good for a young child, but not enough structure could be even worse.

Dealing with the paradox of having strong principles but being able to make compromises for social life is not an easy task, but a necessary and a common fact of life. Nobody likes a bully, but nobody will follow a pushover either.

There is no easy formula for this one – rather it is an on-going process of trial and error, learning from past experiences, and finding the appropriate equilibrium.

8. Be Honest, though not brutally Honest

Honesty is an important virtue, and also a dangerous one. Nobody likes or trusts a liar, but lying is the lubricant that makes social life possible.

We disrespect and disregard liars. And nobody will follow someone who they do not trust and who can betray them at any moment.

But at the same time, people have to live a life in which they recognize other people, and other people's desires and interests. They can't just live for themselves. People who are honest all the time are indifferent to other people. Honesty has a double nature: it makes social things possible, but also makes them impossible. So one of the things that happen is that people have a kind of area for honesty and an area for social lying. It's absolutely necessary. Because life needs to have some padding to be tolerable.

Sometimes to fit into a social situation, people need to pretend to have different feelings than their own. Anybody who goes around telling people the truth all the time is not a welcomed guest and never will be.

9. Handle Awkwardness with Grace

One of the most useful skills in life is being able to handle awkward moments gracefully. Whether it is a miscommunication, clumsiness or just a strange discomfort, awkward moments are just an unavoidable byproduct of social life. Dealing with awkwardness gracefully it is not a common notion, and we often lack the tools to do it. However, being aware of it, and having the ability to handle it gracefully, will put people at ease and will often stop further awkwardness/complication. Just like an experienced driver carries a spare tire and a jack for a possible flat tire, the experienced manager should carry with him "extra gracefulness" for those moments of social discomfort.

10. Make People Happy with gifts from the heart!

The ability to give joy is one of the most useful tools in life, and learning how to make a balloon flower is a simple and powerful way to give joy. The balloon may only last a few hours or a few days, but the memories and good feelings from it will last far into the future.

Balloon flower instructions:

1. Inflate two 5" balloons and tie them together
3. Tie two new balloons as in steps 1, but to this tie a third balloon.
4. Hold the two sets close to each other at the knots, bring the knots to touch each other and twist the two sets together, randomly as if tossing a salad.
5. Inflate two more balloons of a different color with less air, and tie them together.
6. Twist the third set into the first two sets.
7. Put the two new balloons opposite of each other and organize the original 5 balloons around them, revealing the shape of the flower (see back cover picture).

Download at www.TheBalancedManager.com

Postscript

The book *The Inflatable Crown* was published by a major publisher with a first printing of 50,000 copies. To learn more, see www.balloonhat.com/inflatablecrown.

Andy Vermouth's documentary movie about the Inflatable Crown project has won awards at several prominent American film festivals. To see a preview, go to www.balloon-hatmovie.com.

Charlie Eckert is now a successful photojournalist whose pictures have appeared on the front page of the *New York Times* and in *Time* Magazine. Among the places he has worked are Afghanistan and Haiti. Learn more at www.CharlesEckert.com.

Sass Somekh, is retired from the semiconductor-equipment industry. In 2007 he co-founded Musea Venture - a venture capital firm dedicated to starting and investing in companies in the areas of alternative energy and synthetic biology. For more, see www.MuseaVentures.com.

Addi Somekh is now a corporate team-building trainer. His consulting firm, Team Building Arts, numbers among its clients the *Oprah* and *Wired* magazines, the Disney ABC Network Group, and the Skirball Cultural Center in Los Angeles. The firm's specialty is the use of art for team and relationship building. For more, see www.TeamBuildingArts.com

Recommended reading

1. Ichak Adizes, *Corporate Lifecycles*
2. Tal Ben-Shahar, *Happier*
3. Dale Carnegie, *How to Win Friends and Influence People*
4. Bruce M. Patton, William L. Ury, and Roger Fisher, *Getting to Yes*
5. Al Ries and Jack Trout, *Positioning*

Notes

Notes

_____

_____

_____

_____

_____

_____

_____

_____

_____

_____

_____

_____

_____

_____

_____

_____

_____

_____

_____

Notes

Notes

Notes

Notes

Notes

Notes

Notes

Notes

Notes

Notes

Notes

Notes

Notes

Notes

20124403R00059

Made in the USA
Charleston, SC
29 June 2013